GO AND PLAY

SQUASH

GO AND PLAY SQUASH

TECHNIQUES AND TACTICS

JAHANGIR KHAN
WITH RICHARD EATON

STANLEY PAUL
LONDON

The author and publisher wish to acknowledge Rahmat Khan who was a co-author of *Winning Squash*, from which this book has been adapted.

Thanks are due to Mary Eaton without whose help the manuscript could not have been produced.

The author and publishers would like to thank Peter Dazeley for his excellent photographs and also Fritz Borchert, Stephen Line, Colorsport and AllSport.

Stanley Paul & Co. Ltd
An imprint of Random Century Group
20 Vauxhall Bridge Road, London, SW1V 2SA

Random Century Australia (Pty) Ltd
20 Alfred Street, Milsons Point, Sydney 2061

Random Century New Zealand Limited
18 Poland Road, Glenfield, Auckland

Random Century South Africa (Pty) Ltd
PO Box 337, Bergvlei 2012, South Africa

First published as *Winning Squash* 1985
This edition 1992

Set in Garamond Light by
SX Composing Ltd, Rayleigh, Essex
Printed and bound in Great Britain by Clays Ltd
A catalogue record for this book is available from the British Library

ISBN 0 09 177193 5

CONTENTS

PREFACE

Not many players transcend their sport. Even fewer do so from a background of ill-health and poverty. Perhaps none have achieved it from a situation in which they were told not to play a game.

Jahangir Khan used to sneak out and hit a ball up against a wall when his father did not know he was doing it. The skinny-looking lad had had a hernia and was thought not to be strong enough for sport. But his strength of mind could not be diagnosed and Jahangir would not be kept away from squash.

Once that became clear his father, Roshan Khan, who had originally hoped the lad might become another great Khan squash player, decided the doctors might have been wrong. Roshan, a British Open champion himself in 1957, had even given Jahangir a name which means Conqueror of the World.

Jahangir managed to become that and more. He had plenty of natural ability. He grew muscular, compact and powerful. With the help of his cousin Rahmat Khan he acquired discipline. He became not only world champion, but the world champion of world champions – in any sport.

Consider his list of achievements. He first won the world title at 17, which made him the youngest champion ever, and he went on to win it a record six times (so far). Jahangir also became the best hardball player in the world, thus mastering different versions of squash on each side of the Atlantic. He became so much a master of the international softball version that he once went five years and seven months and more than 500 matches unbeaten. Nobody in any other sport has achieved that.

When Jahangir's fantastic run was finished, he himself was not. He came back not only to get the better of the tenacious man who finally brought him down, Ross Norman, but of a more dangerous challenger, Jansher Khan, an unrelated namesake who threatened to take over completely for most of 1987. By 1988 Jahangir had become the first player to win the world title back.

There followed the unpredictably brilliant threat of Australian Rodney Martin, perhaps the greatest stroke-player today, whom Jahangir beat in three successive British Open finals. By doing that the Pakistani overtook the record of eight British Opens set up by another remarkable Australian, Geoff Hunt, and went on to extend the list to ten.

In the process Jahangir became the wealthiest, most watched, most travelled, and most written about squash player of all time, and perhaps the greatest of all time, but assuredly the best known. Even those who understand little of squash have usually heard something of Jahangir.

From such difficult beginnings how could he have done this in one of the world's most rapidly spreading sports? Was it the tragedy of Torsam Khan's death on court in Australia in 1979 that charged him to live out his brother's cheated ambition? Was it the pervasive influence of Pakistan's extraordinary traditions in squash? Was it ability inherited from the Khan family that has mysteriously spawned so many champions?

The correct emphasis of all these likely answers will remain one of the curiosities of sport. What is absolutely certain is that Jahangir – conqueror, record-breaker, and reconqueror – has more than justified the name his father gave him. And become a unique sporting legend.

RICHARD EATON
February 1992

Richard Eaton has probably watched more international squash than anybody, having written about the sport for twenty years and travelled extensively in four continents. He earned a blue at squash and tennis, became racket sports correspondent of *The Sunday Times*, and contributed regularly to the BBC World Service. Later he became squash correspondent of the *Independent* and became involved as author, co-author or editor of ten racket sports books, including *Winning Squash* by Jahangir Khan and Rahmat Khan, and *Advanced Squash* by the same authors.

CHAPTER

1 HOW I BECAME WORLD CHAMPION

I was told I would never become world champion. I was the youngest, smallest, feeblest and sickest of the family. Neither the doctor nor my father believed there was any chance for me to become a good squash player. That might sound surprising but it was not at the time. I had two hernia operations by the age of twelve, but all that did was to strengthen my determination.

I still listen to my father and do as he says. If he asks me to wash the car, I do so. In Pakistan we believe in respect for our elders, and that helps supply discipline. It might sound strange to modern Western ears, but discipline and determination can take you a very long way. Most people can acquire these if they really resolve to. They are not expensive. They cannot in any case be bought. I came from a poor family, yet both my father, Roshan, and my elder brother, Torsam, whom I loved and who died, became world class players. I believe my story can offer hope to millions of people all over the world who are poor, bereaved, or sick. At different times I have been all three.

Role of Fantasy

I did, however, have one great advantage. I was a member of the Khan family, the family that has produced so many great players. Some of them I never saw, but no matter. I certainly heard about them and this created seeds which grew in my mind. People think the first lesson begins when you go on to the court, but that is not so. The first lesson is hearing from others what can be achieved. I heard more in my family in a short time than many people hear throughout an entire career.

The next thing you need after discipline and determination, is ambition. When I started going to the Fleet Club in Karachi to play by myself at the age of ten, I used to try to imagine what it was like to be a good player. I thought about it long and hard. I would dream about it while I sat on the toilet, and fantasize about hitting the ball hard to a length or playing a boast. I would make the noise of the ball with my mouth! It may seem childish or ridiculous but it was in fact helping to develop my hopes and my ambition. Top players sometimes go to the toilet for a few minutes before their matches to strengthen their resolution. I really recommend it!

Create the Soil

My father Roshan had been British Open champion, and therefore world number one himself. He told me I could play squash only if I finished my homework first. So I used to do the work in the afternoon before I got home. When my father was away I used to cry and go running to my mother. But quite often my brother Torsam would play with me and help me. I can laugh about all that now.

Of course most people do not have the advantage of being born a Khan, but there are other ways

to create the soil in which the seed of ambition can grow. Those without squash players in their families must go to a club. Parents should take genuinely interested children to a good coach, and perhaps introduce them to tournaments and magazines and books on squash. All this can be done quite easily, and should be far more than it is. It might help to make the world a better place because sport is one of the easiest ways of keeping young people out of trouble. Whatever you put into a child's mind he is likely to use. Put squash there.

Nature Not Nurture

Because I was the weakest member of the family I'm told they took special care of me. Being weak may also have made me quiet, because that's certainly how I was. Some reckon I became, in addition, spoilt. The story goes that I would say: 'I want milk' and be given it. Then I would say, 'I want sugar', and when I was given that too, I would ask, 'Can you take the sugar out?' It sounds selfish, but perhaps it indicated that my will and ambition were growing. After a while, so did my strength. By the time I won the Pakistan junior championship my father and the doctors were beginning to change their minds about my future. I was fitter and stronger than they expected. The feeling was growing that I might have the desire to become a champion.

Where I live there are few ways to become successful. Squash is one of those few ways and being brought up in a situation like that really motivates you. In that way, hardship can actually help. But it certainly isn't necessary to suffer in order to succeed. If you come from a well-off family you can be just as successful. I believe it depends more upon an individual's nature than his social background. Many young tennis players come from rich families, and because success in tennis is what they really desire and because they work at it, they succeed. They must, though, have an intense drive from within. If you have this, then whether or not you are rich doesn't matter.

A champion's smile

My desire to succeed carried me into the Pakistan junior team, to Sweden, and, on the way home, to England to visit my brother Torsam, who was living in London. Torsam invited me to stay, which pleased me greatly. England is where players need to come if they are to improve. The tournaments, the facilities, the competition are all there. Many players, including myself, have decided to live in England for several months in the year. You have a great advantage in squash if you are English.

Unfortunately Torsam's health was not good, and he was well aware of it. But he told no one. Instead, he discussed with my cousin Rahmat how best I should be settled in England, rather than exhausting myself running around the circuits and living in hotels. Torsam arranged for us to have a fifty per cent share in the Dunnings Mill Squash Club in Sussex. A marvellous plan was laid before me. Along with other juniors I was to be taken there to try to create something in squash that was good for everybody. It seemed almost too good to be true, and indeed it was. A few weeks later Torsam was dead.

There are many, many people who know what it is like to suffer hardship, loss and bereavement. Some of them undoubtedly feel their handicaps make it impossible for them to succeed. That is understandable. But I would like to convince them that this is not necessarily true. Just consider for a moment what happened to us.

Tragedy to Overcome

Torsam went to play the Australian circuit and a week later there was a phone call to say that he had had a heart attack. The next day the doctor rang to say there was no hope. The machines that were keeping my brother alive had to be turned off. It was as though some life force within me had been turned off as well.

The day afterwards I flew to Pakistan. I was determined to go even though I was very upset. Torsam's body was flown out a few days later, and that was the worst moment in my life. When the body arrived at the airport the whole family was desolate. My father was shattered. My mother and sister-in-law almost fainted. I hardly knew what was happening.

Lost as we were we obeyed our Muslim tradition in these things. The body was brought to the home, washed and with prayers from the Koran, taken from the house to the cemetery. At this dreadful moment the seed of a new determination was conceived in me to do what Torsam had always wanted, to become world champion. Out of misery was born the vision of a sporting miracle.

Birth of a Partnership

Miracles need earthly interpretation, and the next step was to plan its development. People at home pressurized us to stay in Pakistan, but it was a pressure to be resisted. They wanted Pakistan to have a world champion – without thinking what it is that *makes* a world champion. If you do not have the right coach, conditions and organization, there is no guarantee of success. Some of those people tried every ploy to keep me at home, to the point of irritation. I was even offered a big house complete with servants. Needless to say, a big house does not make a world champion.

Instead I went to live in London with Rahmat who for several years was my coach.

Perhaps it looks now as though it was the obvious thing to take advantage of Rahmat's offer but in fact making the right decision was not easy. Air Chief Marshal Nur Khan, one of the leading figures in sport in Pakistan and a prominent name with Pakistan International Airlines who sponsored me, warned that if we failed, we would be answerable to the nation. A massive responsibility had descended on our shoulders.

We had to do something that none of the great players who had stayed at home – Qamar Zaman, Mohibullah Khan, Gogi Alauddin, Maqsood Ahmed – had been able to do. We had to overcome Geoff Hunt in a world championship, to get the better of the Australian who was fitter than any other player in the world. We could see why; no Pakistani had yet done this. Whether you are a Khan or a magician you cannot show your magic until you reach the ball. I had to go through the sort of training that would leave me with no excuses about lack of fitness. I had to become fitter than any of my compatriots had ever been.

Truth is Hard

Squash players at all levels have to be fitter than ever before. To achieve that they need to be absolutely and completely honest with themselves. I had to have a training target. If I didn't meet it, or couldn't, I had to admit it. There were to be no lies.

That was not easy; it never is. But to begin with it was even harder because I would cry for my brother. I felt a long way from home. One day, I realized I should not cry any more. I must not be weak but instead I should do something for my brother.

Work Destroys Sadness

There were other hardships. It was also hard to get used to a strange country, with a different climate, different food and very different people. The right food is particularly important for a squash player. I also had to learn a new language – English – if I was really to progress in the world of squash. Sometimes I would get homesick. However, I did so much training that by the time I got home I was usually too tired to be unhappy. Despite this, there were times when I felt like packing up.

These sort of things I believe are special tests provided for you. If you face them, and overcome them, they present opportunities to make yourself stronger and better and more successful in life.

I suppose if I had sat around and thought about Torsam's death then I would not have played squash properly any more; or if my father had brooded about the fact that Torsam had had a weak heart, then I might have been afflicted by the same mood, and would not have become world champion. For death there is no answer – unless you have faith. In the same way that the injuries turned my cousin towards coaching I believe that all my disadvantages were a kind of test or a way of guiding me in a certain direction.

Positive Thinking and Faith

I often believe we are in touch with loved ones who have passed on: Rahmat with his father Nasrullah, myself with my brother Torsam. Often I dream about Torsam. Although many may think this strange or silly, it gives me strength. When I get up in the morning and need to work hard, it refreshes me if I have been dreaming this way.

It is not certain what response you will make to a test. It was not certain that I should become world champion: only that a particular route be made available for me to succeed. Not that I thought about failing. Little worse can happen to you than having somebody you love die, and we must not forget that we ourselves have to go through death as well. So we must try to think positively, investing whatever abilities we have in the task. If you are to succeed at squash, try to do the same.

KHAN'S CONQUESTS I

JAHANGIR BEATS GEOFF HUNT:
7-9, 9-2, 9-2, 9-1;
WORLD OPEN FINAL, TORONTO 1981

On November 28, 1981, two years to the day after Torsam died, I became world champion. My brother's great wish had been fulfilled for him. I don't know whether you believe in coincidences but if you do this was a very unusual one. All I can add is that I had been infused with my brother's spirit to do it.

It was six months since my defeat by Geoff Hunt in the British Open. They were months of intense preparation. Rahmat Khan and I went to Gilgit in North Pakistan and did extensive training at a high altitude. Then we went to Sweden and did some more there. Then to Australia. Different atmospheres, different parts of the world and different climates, but the same dedication to strengthen my legs and my mind still further. There were to be no little mistakes at crucial moments a second time, as there had been in the British Open. I was determined that the World Open should be ours.

I would be stretched by having the ball thrown to me in different corners of the court – and I was not allowed to make any mistakes. I counted the strokes of each rally played in practice, often up to a hundred and occasionally two hundred. Not many rallies last that long, even these days. There had been no criticisms at the time of my British Open performance – they were to come after I had had a holiday. When they did come I was just waiting for the spur to get cracking. I worked harder than I'd ever worked before.

Most people are unaware that when the moment came to play the World Open final I did not know whether I was fit enough to take part. I had an injured shoulder, and it was so painful I could not lift the racket above my head. Obviously I did not want to tell anyone because rumours spread, give confidence to opponents and undermine one's own morale. I was afraid to go to the doctor for the same reason.

The day before the final I still could not properly lift my arm up. It is always difficult to make decisions in such circumstances about whether or not to play. I had been competing well enough to reach the final and even to be regarded by the press as slight favourite to take away Hunt's title. Yet I might be risking another defeat in a big final because I was not at my best. Ultimately these decisions depend entirely on your attitude.

My attitude is that, provided the injury does not threaten your career, then sometimes you have to go ahead and struggle on with whatever ailment you have. My father Roshan won a Dunlop Open final when he had lost seven teeth after being struck by a racket. But once on the court any injury had to be forgotten and the mind had to focus on only one thing – getting on with the job.

I decided to do so. I was shown a recording of the British Open final against Hunt, just as a last-minute reminder that I was not to make the same mistakes again. We wanted to try to make Hunt move and to keep him moving. For that reason I did more boasting than before, taking him up and back, up and back, up and back. Hunt responded by striking the ball higher on the front wall and at a slower speed, and even by lobbing. That was worrying because of the possible effect upon my shoulder of having to force the pace. But the match was not to last long enough to make it worse.

The first game occupied about three quarters of an hour. Though I lost it I felt that this time I was on course for victory. That game had taken a great deal out of Hunt. The boasting had taken its toll. Most unusually, he was arguing with the referee by the end of the game, shouting loudly.

Once again, though, I was forced to admire him. I believe that even at this early stage he knew he was beaten, but still tried to keep going. He tried more lobbing, he varied the pace and direction, and conserved every ounce of energy. He was no longer so fast but he was looking for ways to overcome it.

Though I lost the first game I still had to go on playing the same way. Early in the second Hunt again shouted at a refereeing decision, and threw his racket down. Hunt is normally quiet, and this was a clear and obvious sign he was not comfortable. Though it was hard to believe, I had to make sure I didn't let up. At the end of the second game Hunt was unable to play the last two rallies. The same happened at the end of the third. The end was near.

I had to go on court and put everything out of my mind just one more time. There was little chance of Hunt recovering. He was exhausted. But I still paid him the compliment of putting everything into it. This time I needed to finish the job like a professional.

When it happened Rahmat and I knelt on the court in prayer. This wasn't planned, it occurred naturally. I didn't know anything about the noise going on around or notice that all the spectators were standing. I wasn't even really aware of my own feelings. In a way it hurts because such moments are so fleeting – here briefly, and gone. If you are like me, you thank the creator who put you in that situation. That helps you to learn from both victory and defeat. Then even though the goal may have been achieved the success will not go to your head.

Lesson Victory is a great thing – see that your head is not.

CHAPTER

2

STARTING

If a child is to succeed at squash, or anything in life, much depends on the relationship with the parents. Discipline is esential because standards have risen tremendously. The first discipline is respect for parents. The second is to play regularly, and the third is to go through the punishment and pressure of training. If the child has respect for parents, he or she is more likely to have respect for the coach, and for the work schedule.

Parents should decide where the child's possible talent lies, then apply him or her to that with all the necessary encouragement. I believe many more parents should be encouraging their children towards sport to keep them free of bad influences. A child should not be left to make important decisions before he is ready. There are many opportunities for corruption.

Respect for Authority

In Pakistan, father and family have more authority than they do in the West. We also believe in unity and loyalty. If my father were to ring and say he wanted to see me the next day, that would be it; no question of excuses as to why I could not come, world champion or not. I see little of this kind of relationship in England.

In the West, parents sometimes feel that they should allow independence to their offspring while they are still children. But if a child is going wrong, this is no good. He has to learn not to play with fire. An adult, by reason of experience, usually knows more about life, society, and what is good for a youngster. Therefore I think an adult should make the decision as to whether or not the child should play squash seriously, and the decision should be accepted. Similarly, if you are young and know little about the game, yet question the authority and views of the coach, it is likely he will refuse to teach you. Even when you do not agree you should have enough respect to listen.

Careful Shopping

Whether as a child or an adult, before starting to play you should speak to a coach about buying a racket. It is easy to use one that is wrong for you. Testing the size, weight and feel is like shaking hands – some people squeeze, some don't. Some do it nice and gently so you feel there is no effort, others crush it. If the racket feels comfortable when you swing it, then it may be the right one. Usually it is best to choose a well-known brand.

It is helpful to have two rackets if you can afford them. You might lose one or break the strings. Breakage of strings is a hazard which can be reduced by using a racket cover when not playing. That acts as a protection from the weather and wet clothes. The cover can also be used for storing money, watch, and valuables and taken on court with you.

A racket handle is very important. Some people use a leather grip, which looks nice, but a little sweat will make it slippery and dangerous. I recommend a towelling grip or any of the new types of material which absorb perspiration. The handle must be kept dry. A grip should be changed frequently because a dirty one becomes shiny and can fly out of the hand.

Choosing Equipment

A wrong size grip can send the racket flying. There should be half a finger's width or less between the end of the fingers and the palm of the hand when it is wrapped around the racket. Test it carefully.

A bumper strip around the top of the head is often on graphite and metal rackets. The rules say it is dangerous if the bumper strip is broken, which may happen after it comes into contact with walls. Check it and change it immediately if necessary.

I used to think that despite the development of graphite rackets, only wooden frames provided the feeling for the ball that was needed. But the range of synthetic materials has increased so much, and their sensitivity has improved so much more than expected, that almost everybody uses them now. They provide far more power and permit bigger heads which enlarge the sweet spot in the centre of the strings. They also make greater demands upon the buyer to research carefully which is the most suitable racket for him or her. Greater demands, but greater possibilities too.

It is not necessary to start with strings of top quality natural gut. Natural gut is important for a stroke player, or for someone who slices the ball a lot. But gut breaks more easily than synthetic strings. If you are a beginner or someone who usually hits the ball flat, you may be wasting your money. If you don't drive at a 100 miles per hour you don't need a Porsche.

Importance of Clothing

Proper clothing is essential. Don't go on court in a rugby shirt, or jeans, or anything other than nice clean squash gear. It will make you feel better about yourself. For men, suitable shorts are especially important. Squash shorts, unlike tennis shorts, should stretch, and will be lighter because they are shorter. Beware of any material that *becomes* heavy as the game goes on. I once knew a player who played a long, sweaty match in shorts with a towelling panel down the side. The towelling grew so heavy with sweat that the shorts started to fall down in the middle of an important rally!

No need to spend a lot. But it is more important in squash than most sports to get clothing just right – something that gives freedom of movement and is clean. Squash is one of the few strenuous exercise sports in which you are close to your opponent most of the time. Imagine if your fiancée bumped into you during a rally. It could be the end of a beautiful relationship!

For similar reasons, always carry a towel with you. It may be necessary to dry yourself between games. It can also become important to mop perspiration off the floor. Many floors are wax sealed. This makes them more slippery because the sweat is not absorbed.

Beware of the Feet

A most important item is the shoe. Many people buy plain footwear, such as jogging shoes, or tennis shoes, but these are made for those specific activities. Squash has different movements. The sole of a jogging shoe is too high for squash. It may look nice, but if you turn sideways, or if you jump and come down on the high heel, then your ankle may turn. Then you could suffer unnecessary injury.

The sole of the shoe is also important. You need a good grip on the floor, even more grip than on a tennis shoe, in order to thrust off and change direction quickly. Without this you can easily slip. Some shoes have long laces. If so, tie them two or three times, because if they flop about this is far more dangerous than people realize.

Rahmat and Jahangir with the ideal equipment

The shoe must not be heavy, or ankles may become weak and unstable. Stand on one foot. If this makes the leg tremble then the ankle and shoe together are not strong enough. The ankle needs enough support at the back to stop the wobbling which affects the knee, the back and the whole body.

The punishment the feet get during training and whilst playing is considerable, so it is useful for socks to have a cushion. This affects the whole foot, and probably ligaments in the leg too. Blisters are a problem which may hinder you if you are not careful. To try to prevent them some players use double socks, which I believe is potentially dangerous. If the inside sock gets wet while the outside sock stays dry, one will move inside the other. That causes further stress on the ankle.

Avoiding Injuries

A most valuable piece of equipment is a tracksuit. If the weather is cold, then the tracksuit is obviously necessary, but perhaps more important it helps you to warm up properly. Then you can stretch without risk of injury. At the end of a match put the track suit on again to help you warm *down*. In between, if you put the track suit top on, take your shirt off. Wet clothes are unhealthy. For this reason a kitbag needs different compartments for damp clothes. Some people use separate small bags, but it is worth getting a nice big one. Then, provided your racket has a cover, it too can go inside.

One final item that I would like to see used more is eyeguards. These are obligatory in Canada, but rarely (at the time of writing) even used in other parts of the world. I am in favour of them because there are probably more serious eye injuries in squash than any comparable bat and ball game. The situation is nowhere near dangerous enough to stop anyone playing: the rules are designed to protect you. But I believe eyeguards can be important for lower grade players among whom more of the serious injuries occur.

It is possible the Canadian attitude to safety in squash will spread and I hope it does. It is also likely that the designs of eyeguards will improve.

When to Start

There is no reason why you should not start playing as soon as you can hold a racket. My niece Natasha started when she was only four-and-a-half. She simply held the racket and tried to make contact with the ball. The ball was on the floor: she would not have hit it had it been bouncing, but this didn't matter. She was learning to strike it in the right direction.

Training is a different matter. When to start will depend on the child's physical development, and if you are helping a young beginner, assessing this physical development accurately is vital if you want the child to be disciplined and able to go through the pressures of training. No youngster should be going on long runs at the age of nine or ten. He or she needs to be a little bit grown up for that, perhaps fifteen years old.

Whether you are young or old when you begin you need help, and you need to join a club. It may seem obvious to say so, but it is worth ensuring that the club is reasonably close. If you are always in danger of being late then you are inflicting unnecessary pressure on yourself, though it's remarkable how many squash players do that.

Read the rules and go to a professional coach. It is a false economy to seek the help of a friend: he or she may not know how to teach properly. Playing without proper tuition can cause injuries. For this reason make sure you understand the rules, especially those relating to fair view of the ball and excessive swing. If you don't contain your swing, and if you don't learn where you are permitted to stand in relation to your opponent and the ball, then someone will get hit. That can be extremely serious.

How a Child Starts

If you have a child who wants to start, give him (or her) a ball and put him on a squash court. Let him hit the ball around the floor like a hockey player. This helps build up both enthusiasm and control. You can even kick the ball back to him. Talk to him or her. Encourage a confident attitude. Point out pictures of the top players in the newspapers. Read to them. Show them films.

Youngsters should be fed the ball underarm from six or eight feet away. Stand on one side of the court with the child on the other and ask him to hit it into your hands. That builds up control and accuracy. Then play the ball to him with the racket.

Cut down the handle of the child's racket if necessary. Always give equal importance to forehand and backhand.

Some beginners have a backhand weakness, and as in tennis, there are coaches who allow beginners to hit the backhand with two hands. I do not advise it, even as a temporary measure. Eventually in squash it has to be given up. That means you will have to do twice the work.

Grips, Conventional and Unorthodox

The most used grip is the 'shakehands' (see photo 1). For that you put three fingers together and the index finger further forward, with a gap between it and the middle finger (see photo 2). The thumb, on the other side of the handle, is placed in a position between the middle and index fingers (see photo 3). You can practise it. Whenever you see an object of a similar shape to a racket handle, pick it up. A child can sometimes do it with a toy. Learning can occur without pressure.

My grip is different. For me it is better than the shakehands grip and I also recommend it for other players. What I do is to twist the racket round slightly, perhaps an eighth of the way round in a clockwise direction. The racket turns, but not the grip (photo 4). Doing this opens the face of the racket on the forehand – which is the recommended advice for hitting the forehand with the other grip anyway, except that you use the wrist. My grip brings a little natural slice to the forehand, which is also desirable. Most of all it gives much more control on the backhand and on volleys. Both are regarded as my strong shots and I am certain the grip helps. Another major point about gripping the racket is that it can be quite a disadvantage if you allow the head of the racket to drop. It may well make you slower in your preparation for your strokes. *Don't*, though, use a grip further round in an anti-clockwise direction from the shakehands (photo 5). You are then holding the racket like a meat-axe.

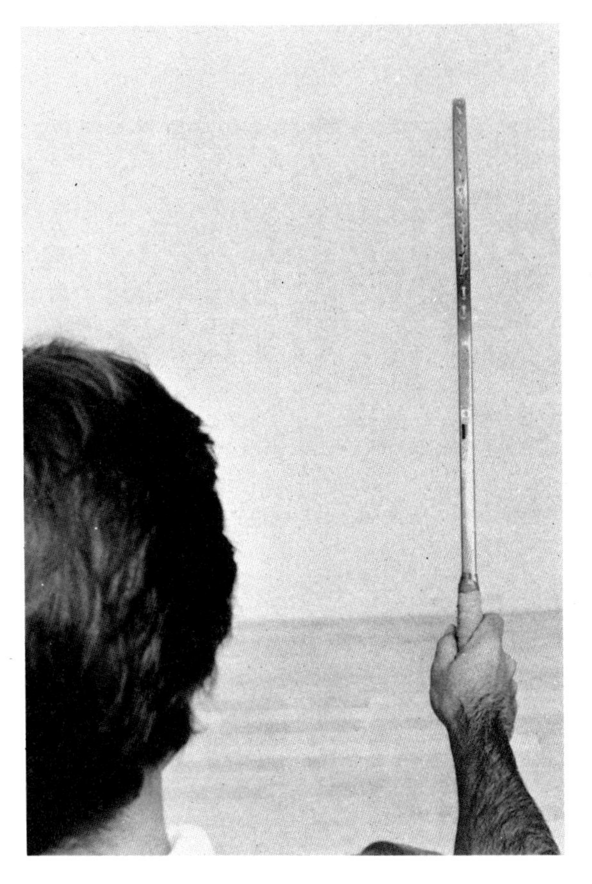

1. Conventional grip Sometimes called the 'shakehands grip'. Shake hands with the racket so that left hand top edge of shaft goes into the 'V' between thumb and forefinger

With my grip, the forehand becomes slightly like holding a spoon. The backhand is not nearly as open – in fact the racket is almost perpendicular. (Compare it in photo 6 with the other grips, photos 7 and 8.) The wrist can be used to tilt it slightly back, but not too much. It gives more thumb behind the handle, especially on the backhand drop. The grip is very good for this shot but quite satisfactory too for a hard length shot, which you will find you hit almost flat. With the shake-

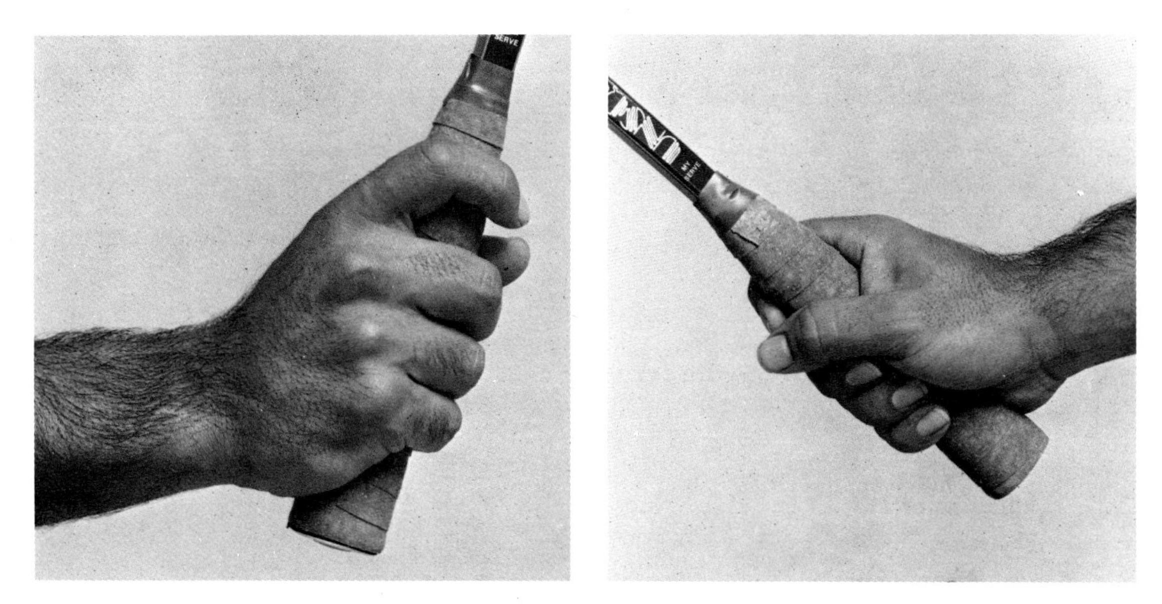

2. The grip from the back Note position of forefinger, and the gap between forefinger and middle finger

3. The grip from the front Three fingers come round to the front of the handle with the thumb in between the middle finger and forefinger

4. Jahangir Khan grip Turn the racket a little in a clockwise direction from the conventional grip. Better for the backhand and good for a slightly sliced forehand drive

5. Incorrect grip Racket turned too far in an anti-clockwise direction. Will cause weak backhand and an insensitive grip

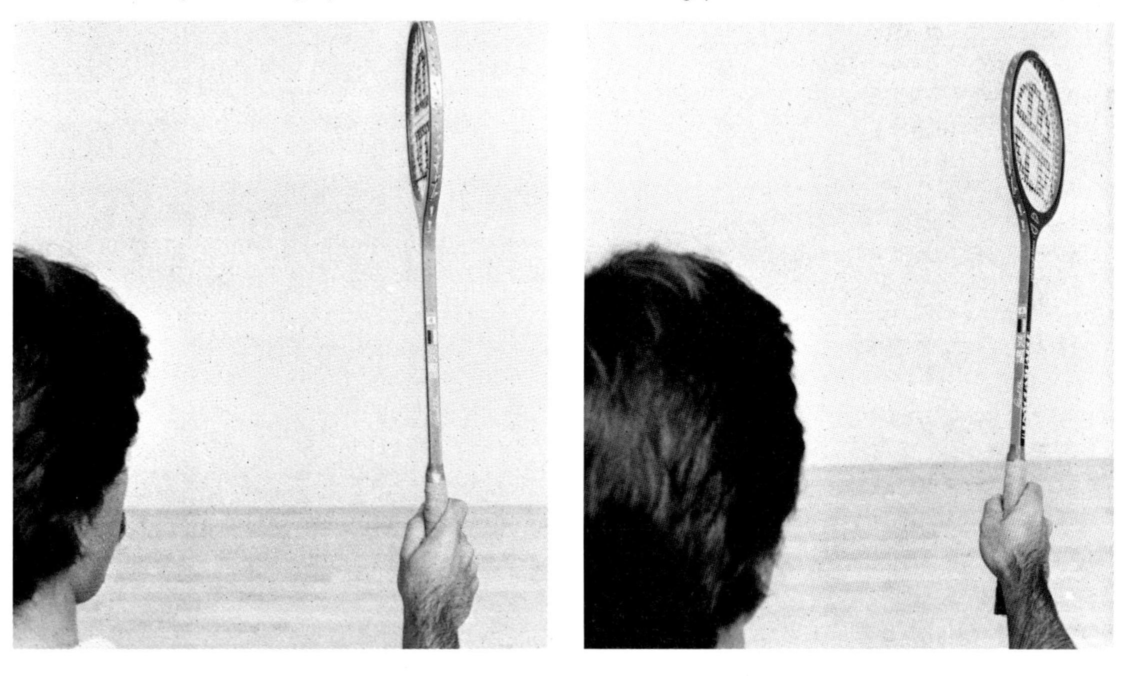

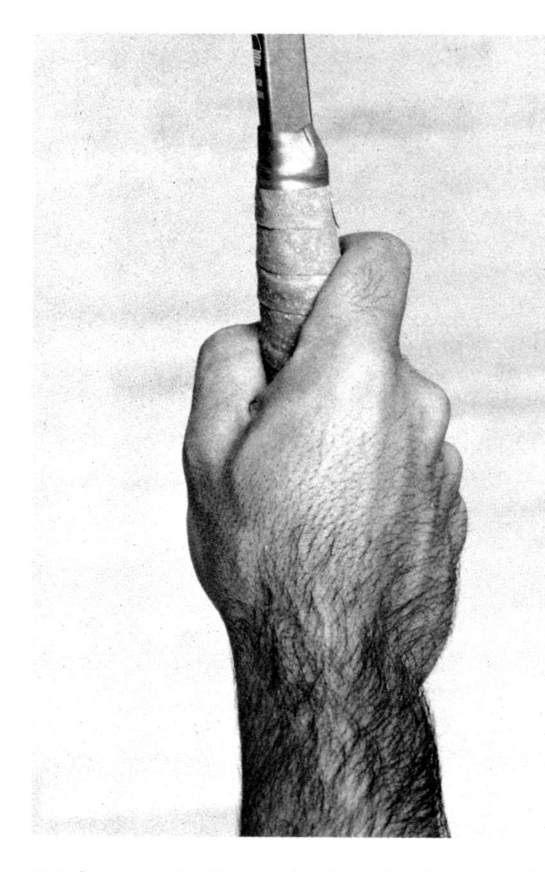

6. Jahangir grip close up Leading edge of racket shaft has just become visible

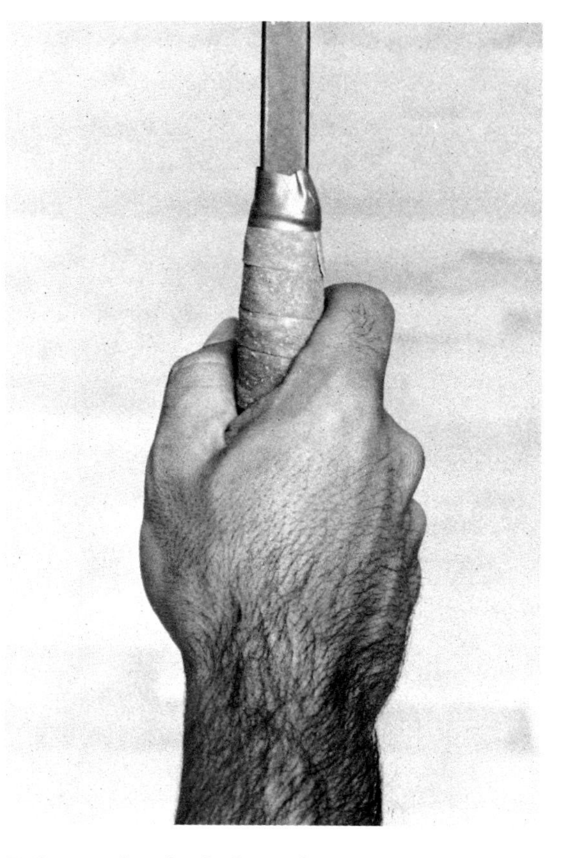

7. Conventional grip from close up Note position of 'V' of forefinger and thumb

hands grip there tends to be more slice on the backhand drive, which may diminish its power. Mine is a perfect grip for a volley drop shot, and I believe that by adopting it you open the door to more progress in several areas.

For instance, you can hit a forehand drive quite well with my grip, but I don't believe you can hit any backhand shot so well with the shakehands. On the backhand volley with the latter you are told to bend the wrist back so that the racket face becomes more open. That's not too bad for the cross-court volley but the down-the-wall shot can be very difficult. You may have to compensate by putting the wrist in front of the racket, which is an ugly, awkward position. Some books have even illustrated this horrible shot but I believe my way is better for most people.

If you want to change grips as tennis players do, you need to hold the racket at the neck with the left hand. But I don't recommend changing grip, and certainly not in the middle of a rally. Qamar Zaman used to hold the racket at the neck with his left hand, but that is because he used a lot more wrist than most people and he therefore needed to keep checking to see that his grip was exactly right. I never do this. By all means find what suits you best, but generally speaking that should not be too far from the grip that I use.

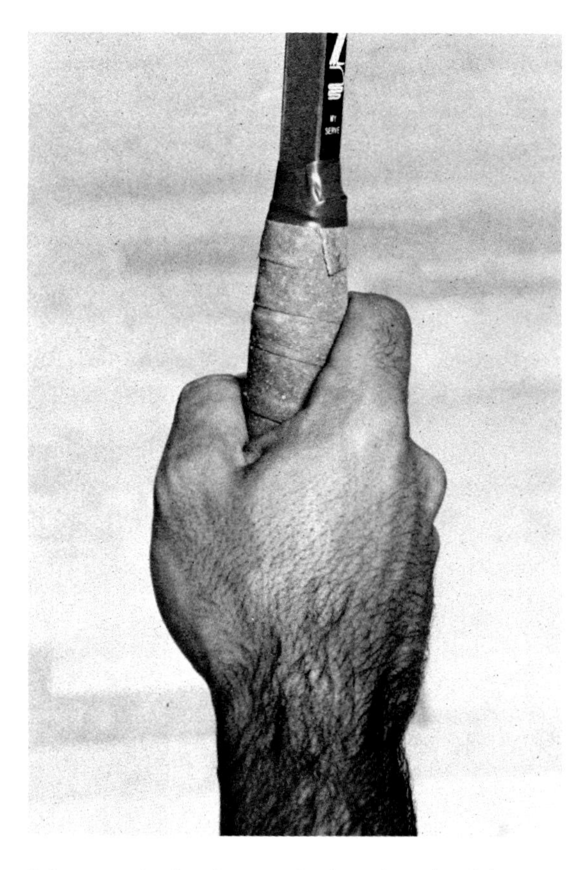

8. Incorrect grip close up See how the palm of the hand lies flat on the back of the handle

Feel and Footwork

Almost as important as grip is 'feel'. The racket should feel comfortable. The fingers and hand should be sensitive to the equipment they are wielding, so that each becomes an extension of the other. You should be able to swing the racket with comfort and control. Do this before you hit the ball. Practise both backhand and forehand, hitting air.

Next, learn a little about basic footwork, enough to know you should be roughly sideways to play a shot, and that power comes from turning the shoulder towards the ball. It is better to have a demonstration or an image of somebody playing the stroke correctly before attempting it yourself. Copying is an excellent method of learning. This way you are likely to get less wrong. Learning can then happen immediately without lengthy descriptions of wrist and preparation, swing and follow-through. Application of talent may require no analysis.

A demonstrated image is also valuable because when you ask young children to hit the ball they sometimes send it into the floor. That can cause trouble. The Egyptian Gamal Awad once told a hilarious story about when he was young and went to a professional to learn golf. 'Let's see how you do it first,' said the pro. 'Here's the club. Show me how you would hold it.' Gamal picked up the club and held it perfectly, feet apart, nice balance. 'Don't tell me you haven't played before,' said the pro. 'I haven't,' said Gamal. The pro was amazed by the perfect stance and grip. 'O.K,' he said, eyes shining with anticipation. 'Here is the ball and now I want you to hit it.' There was a pause. Gamal slowly lifted the club over his head like a hammer and smashed the ball into the ground! The pro nearly died laughing.

Care must be taken over instruction. I've seen a coach stand a beginner near the service box, tell him he was going to throw the ball and ask him to hit it on to the wall. Obediently the beginner stood in position for the forehand. The coach, standing behind him, gently threw the ball intending the pupil to hit it on to the front wall. Instead he delivered a tremendous backhand clout in totally the opposite direction, nearly carrying the coach with it towards the back wall! The lesson is to organize things carefully when you begin. It can be unexpectedly dangerous.

Early Tips

Frequent shortcomings with the first movement of the racket are a floppy wrist or an erratic swing. With a child it is often the case that the racket head is closed – that is, the wrist is turned over so that the racket is connecting with the top of the ball, hitting it into the floor. Sometimes this is because the wrist is not strong enough to keep it firm. But sometimes the child does not realize which part of the ball should be struck.

This is why it is valuable for a youngster to hit the ball about the floor hockey-style. This exercise teaches contact with the back of the ball. The perfect place is slightly to the bottom and to the back. This can be achieved if the ball is hit at the right moment in its flight. That is after the ball has bounced, gone up and is about to come down again. As it begins to drop a second time it travels more slowly and is a more comfortable height.

Don't turn the racket face too open (i.e. tilted backwards) unless you are trying to deliver a high service striking the front wall one foot below the out line. Start with a racket face not far from perpendicular, and aim to hit the ball just above the service line (the middle line). Coaches sometimes talk a lot about what to do with the racket face and not enough about what part of the ball to hit (see diagram). A little shot just above the tin requires the racket to go underneath the ball. A volley often requires you to hit more of the top of it. Better to be concerned about these things rather than what is happening to the racket face.

To start with, hit the back of the ball. Even an adult beginner might do well to practise with the ball on the floor, flicking it as if with a hockey stick. Then try rolling the ball on to the racket and picking it up without touching it with the other hand. Then take the ball and bounce it softly on the racket, up and down, up and down, as many times as possible. This will teach you to keep your eyes on the ball, which is of basic importance at all levels of the game. Having practised hitting the bottom, do a similar exercise hitting the top, bouncing the ball down and up from the floor as many times as you can. Then learn to hit it on the left side of the ball to the right hand wall. Do all these exercises before trying to hit the ball. They help build up control. Too many beginners just go on the court and try to hit it hard straight away. Not many succeed. Don't run before you can walk.

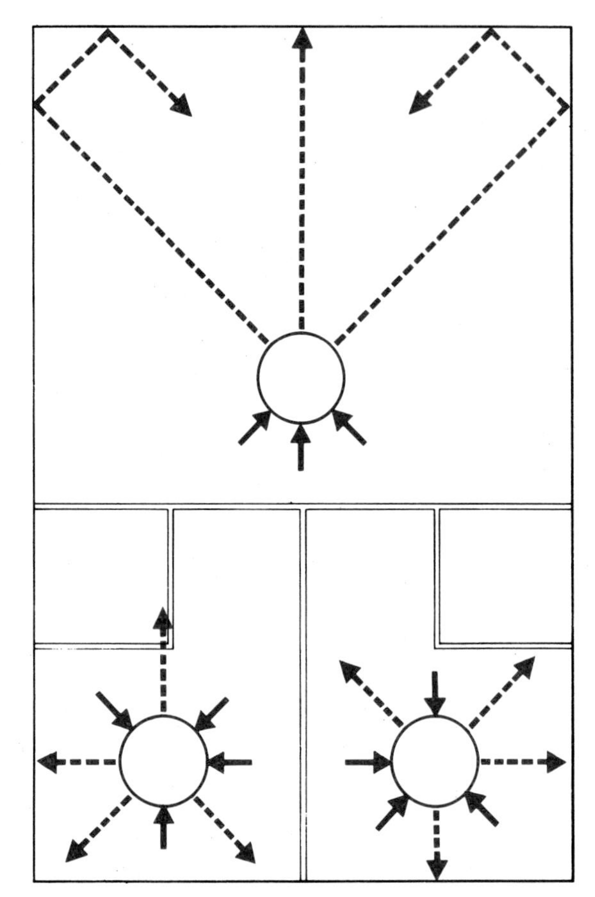

Diagram 1. Learn to hit different parts of the ball, and learn what the outcome will be each time

First Shots

If you have never played it is usually difficult to control the ball when hitting from the back of the court. Don't try. Move close to the front wall, if necessary only a couple of yards away, and flick the ball slowly on to the wall. Don't be embarrassed by the simplicity of the exercise. After you can do this, take a step back and try again. Either hit the ball harder or higher to get extra distance. It may not seem exciting, but you will be learning vital lessons about the height, trajectory, and power of a shot. Keep doing this, moving back, till you are right at the back of the court. Then you will be hitting a length – the most important thing in squash. After that, allow the ball to go past you, and take it off the back wall. This is sometimes difficult for beginners. But don't give up, keep trying. Spend an equal amount of time doing the same exercises on the backhand as well.

A great difficulty is often in hitting the ball off the back wall. Players sometimes move too close so there is no room to swing. Some go too close to the side wall so there is no room there either, and some start breaking rackets. Don't get close to any of the walls. You should be able to stretch your arm right out and only just touch the wall with your racket. Only occasionally should you go closer to the back wall – perhaps, for instance, if you have to retrieve a very good length shot.

All these exercises should be done before starting to think about details of stroke technique. You can create a good substitute for a game with competitions against yourself, seeing how many times you can perform each task. A professional can also throw or feed the ball far more frequently and accurately than any player will ever return the ball in a game. This can help you to play a shot twenty times without a mistake, then fifty, and so on. As this happens, your pleasure in playing will be all the greater. Then the coach can see if you can control where your shot bounces. This affects how and where your opponent can play his own shot, and how much you stretch him. The best practice is to hit the ball up and down the side wall and make it bounce near the service box. This makes it hard for the opponent to cut the ball off on the volley.

Swatting a Fly

One technical defect to eradicate is a big tennis swing. This is not only ineffective but extremely dangerous. You could easily hit your opponent with a backswing or follow-through. Please note that a squash swing and a tennis swing are quite different. A tennis ball is heavy and needs a large arc on the stroke to propel it, often with topspin. A squash ball needs a shorter stroke, perhaps with a little underspin or slice to control it. Imagine swatting a fly. You stop the hitting motion not too long after impact. Then you bring the shot back slightly. A squash forehand is also completely different from a tennis shot because it is more like a throwing action than a swing. Indeed you need to be able to throw properly to play the shot properly. If you can't, then you must practise throwing a ball.

After you have learnt all this, try hitting the ball into the side walls (called boasting) and then start to develop cross-court shots as well. Learn the geometry of squash (see diagram 1). Do these with similar exercises as before. After that, either you or the coach can throw the ball on to the front wall in order to make you play the same shots while moving to them. Preferably you will move from the 'T' in the middle of the court to the ball and back again each time.

It is a lot of hard work. But for that reason it is more satisfying if you manage it. In any case it is the only way to succeed. Only after you have completed all that has been described should you consider the technical matters of how a squash stroke is produced.

KHAN'S
CONQUESTS II

JAHANGIR BEATS GAMAL AWAD:
9-10, 9-7, 9-6, 9-4;
PATRICK INTERNATIONAL FESTIVAL FINAL, CHICHESTER
1983

This was the longest match in the history of squash – two hours and forty-six minutes – and the arguments to which it gave rise were in keeping with the length of the match. Not all that was said was complimentary. There were those who thought the patient rallies and persistent struggle were too demanding of similar qualities in an audience. I don't agree.

I thought the match was good for squash. Certainly we don't need long drawn-out repetitive matches very often, though I don't believe that happens anyway. This particular match was long and drawn out, but because it was so unusual it provided a great deal for people to talk about. That we *do* need.

Plenty of talk had gone on before the match as well. Gamal Awad had been saying he was the only player who could beat me. He also said he was ready to do it. He had trained very hard, and could last a long match, and of course he also possessed his phenomenal speed. But except for the four-game match in the World Open in Toronto eighteen months before, he had not really pushed me very close. This time he did.

I went 8-1 up in the first game and at that stage there was no sign of the colossal struggle to follow. Had I finished that game off there and then I believe it might also have been a quick and straightforward match. Instead, as all people do from time to time, I made mistakes, probably due to lack of concentration. Gamal went quickly to 6-8 and I began to feel a little negative. All of a sudden I was not playing any strokes, but producing a long, safe game. That gave Gamal more chance of getting into the match.

He began rallying up and down, up and down with more determination than I have ever seen in him. He refused to make mistakes, and he would not give way. He was, as usual, very quick on to the ball but, worryingly, also managing to save some of his energy. He had never done that before. It made him much more dangerous. I did not seem to be able to put him under pressure. Gamal went from 6-8 to 8-8 and although I had game balls at 9-8 and 9-9, he had seen his chance and was not to be denied. He took the first game 10-9. I was disappointed.

It was difficult to understand how I could go so far ahead and let it slip. There was much more involved than just this match. It was necessary to consider the consequences for the British Open, which was coming up the following week. I did not want to risk going back on court and taking chances on something silly happening in the second game. It might give Gamal the impression that I would not necessarily beat him at a long game. I set out to dispel that impression. But it meant winning the hard way.

I would have to go on and play just such a long game, with lots of long, safe rallies and wear Gamal down. My plan was the same as that in the Pakistan Open final, when I beat Qamar Zaman for the first time. This is not my natural style – I like to play a harder hitting game and produce some strokes. But stroke-play, when a game down to an encouraged and determined Gamal Awad, was not wise.

Some critics said that I was sucked into playing Awad's way, into playing a negative game, but that is not really so. This may have happened in the first game after I had failed to finish it off, but not in the second, third and fourth. In these games it was my deliberate decision to play that way.

After I had won the second game I thought I would be all right, but I was surprised at how much longer it went on. We often had rallies of 150

strokes and neither of us was prepared to take the risk of injecting any pace into them. After two hours thirty-three minutes we beat the previous world record, a five-game match between Murray Lilley, once of New Zealand and later of Canada, and England's Barry O'Connor.

Despite this, I believe I won the fourth game fairly convincingly. Though I was more tired than at any time since the 1981 British Open final against Geoff Hunt, Awad was exhausted. I was pleased to have won, naturally, but I was particularly pleased to have won it in this way. I had thoroughly tested my fitness for the first time since 1981. I had helped break three records: the longest first game, the longest match, and (almost certainly) the longest rally. And I had destroyed Awad. In the World Open later the same year he got only one point from me. He never came back. That was the end of him as a rival.

Lesson Be prepared to change your tactics if the situation demands it.

CHAPTER

3

HITTING

Only after preparing thoroughly as indicated in chapter two should you think more technically about how to hit the ball. If you have followed my advice you will not yet have grooved any shots. But if you are not to make unnecessary hard work for yourself you should now start to analyse what you are doing right and wrong. Leave it too long and bad habits can become a burden difficult to unload.

Good strokes need good preparation. The first basic stroke is the forehand and for that you should take the racket back as early as possible to give yourself a chance of producing it easily and calmly. Coaches sometimes say you should take the racket up, but I believe it better to say that the racket should be taken back and the arm taken up. When the arm gets above the shoulder, with the elbow bent, then you have maximum strength for a forehand drive (see photo 9).

Maybe this is what coaches mean, but often that is not what they say. Provided the arm gets into that high position, the racket can either be held vertically or tilted in a forward direction. It *is* possible to lift the racket without lifting the arm – and that is the point, because that is exactly what you do not want. Look at photo 10.

As it comes down the racket makes a half circle – like a half moon – and descends to contact the ball at about knee level (photo 11). That's the ideal height when you first learn the shot. In a rally in a match you will inevitably strike it at different heights. But to develop and practise the shot properly you'll need to be bending, and it's best to hit it at knee height. As you take the racket back your weight will be mainly on the right foot, although in some situations the balance may need to be on both feet. When the ball is hit, the weight is always transferred on to the front foot – the left foot for the right-hander.

There is another point coaches sometimes overlook. Make sure to hit the right part of the ball. If

9. Forehand drive preparation Elbow up. Left shoulder and arm pointing down

you are hitting at about knee height, and if you are aiming for somewhere near the service line, impact should be slightly underneath it. When you make contact with the ball, press it. This is shown on the backhand in photo 27. Press on to the target, don't slash at it. I will use the example of the billiard table. The cue goes straight towards where you want the ball to go. In the same way the racket must press through, straight, for at least one foot beyond the ball before completing a natural follow-through.

10. Forehand drive – wrong preparation Right shoulder and elbow down. This will cause a restricted shot

11. Forehand drive – impact (below left) Racket comes down in half circle. Weight on leading foot. Eyes on ball

12. Forehand drive – follow-through (below right) Racket head still under control

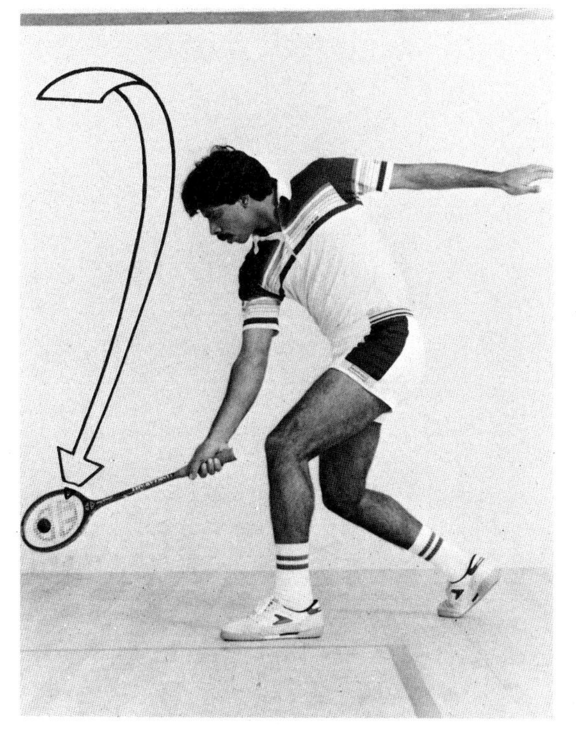

Pressing the Ball

You should be concerned about avoiding an excessive swing on the follow-through. That is wrong and it is dangerous. However, if you concentrate on pressing the ball to the target, the follow-through will tend to stop itself (photo 12). It is as if a piece of elastic is tied to your hand. After you have pressed the racket towards the target, the elastic will bring the arm back. If you do not think about this and practise it, then your racket could be flying everywhere when you hit the ball.

This may sound as though you are not hitting the ball hard. It's not so. You can hit hard and press at the same time. Then you may not even have to worry about what happens on the follow-through. It tends to happen naturally depending on how the arm is built and moves. No two people have the same swing, because no two have an identical build. But remember: if you press on to the ball and into the follow-through there should be a little jerk in your arm which brings the racket back slightly as it finishes the shot.

There is another useful point about doing this correctly. By getting the follow-through right sometimes you don't need much of a backswing. There may not always be time to lift the arm right up as the ball comes quickly to you in a rally. No matter. With a short swing and that pressing motion you can still obtain enough power, as well as a good deal of accuracy. Even if you are flying through the air off the floor, the correct follow-through will send the ball in the right direction.

Wrist Or No Wrist

How much wrist you use in your strokes depends entirely upon the situation. To a certain extent it is also a matter of style. If you concentrate on keeping your grip firm, then what the wrist does tends to happen naturally. Tighten the fingers, but don't stiffen the grip. If this is done the right way, the muscles in the wrist become tight enough to cope with shots close to the tin, where you can afford nothing loose. However, if it comes naturally to a player to use the wrist, then he should do so. If he has wrists that instinctively produce disguise and deception, then he is a lucky player, and he should make use of his luck.

There is, though, a time to use the wrist and a time not to. If the ball has gone past your body you may be forced to use the wrist. Look at photos 13 and 14, and compare 14 on the forehand with 14a on the backhand. Otherwise for a beginner it is, on balance, better to keep the wrist tight, especially

13. Forehand cross court from behind body – impact Wrist compensates for taking ball late. 'Wrong' footwork – right foot in – enables ball to be hit across court: the body does not obstruct

14. Forehand down wall from behind body – impact Compare angle of the wrist with the forehand cross court. The body may hide the direction of both shots from the opponent

14a. Backhand down the wall from behind the body Ball is hit slightly upwards. Notice angle of the wrist, compensating for a late take

for a drop shot or a volley. If you concentrate on the grip, and playing to a good length, a cocked wrist should tighten of its own accord. But when you are trying to deceive your opponent as to where you are going to put the ball, it is the wrist that will send him the wrong way.

Don't worry too much about all this. Often the best way becomes obvious as a matter of common sense. In squash, as in tennis, there was a time when people dressed differently and did not move about so much. Times have altered. Things happen more quickly on court. If you start thinking too much about a stiff wrist, or the right footwork or anything else, you won't be able to do very much with the ball. Many top players play shots off the wrong foot, with and without wrist, and in a hundred different ways. It is important to try to start in the right way, but once a player has developed control he can play pretty well any way he likes.

Forehand and Backhand Differences

However, to begin with you need to know that there are basic differences in the preparation of the backhand and forehand drives. They also share the characteristic that by getting the shoulder towards the ball you create a greater area in which the racket can swing. Let's look at the forehand first.

If the ball is in front of you I suggest you put your left foot forward. That should give you better balance. Follow through by transferring your weight on to that foot. You will be able to bend down better to the shot and press the racket on to the ball more easily. To gain extra power turn your left shoulder so that you are almost looking at the ball over that shoulder. Try pointing with your left forefinger at the line of the ball as it comes to you. Have another look at photo 9.

All these things enable the racket to be taken back, right back, round behind the body, then round to the side where you make contact with the ball, and then round to the front where you follow through. Such a swing is very large, but provided the opponent is not near you it will not be excessive. It is like kicking a ball. For a really powerful kick you take your leg right back.

Three Teaching Aids

If you don't turn the left shoulder to the ball, the right shoulder is immediately behind you and therefore in the way. Then you may have a restricted swing that can become a jab. Perhaps you should even half turn your back to the front wall and point your shoulder forty-five degrees to the side wall. The right shoulder then comes out of a restricting position and faces the back. The left shoulder and left arm point straight towards where you make contact with the ball. People often say you stand sideways to hit the ball but in fact you don't.

This preparation will enable body swivel to come into the shot. To do this you need to be able to turn freely from the hips and you need a flexible trunk. The feet should not move or you may spoil your balance. Try to reach the ball and then stop. Then turn the upper part of your body.

Coaches usually tell you to get the racket back, but frequently fail to say, 'Get the shoulders round'. Better to think of *this*, just as it is better to think of getting the arm up rather than the racket. Likewise it is better to be told to press the ball on to the target rather than to hit it into the back corner. These three important aids are often not taught at all.

The backhand drive is different in that the elbow should be pointing downwards as you prepare. With the forehand drive it points upwards. It is different, too, in that the body is behind the racket arm, not in front of it. Therefore it can get in the way. If you have time and room, rid yourself of this obstruction by getting round quickly.

It does at the same time, however, provide you with a special advantage on the backhand. The body can be used to hide the hand and wrist, and it is possible therefore to mask or disguise a backhand far more effectively than a forehand. Given a ball on the backhand in the front court, you can show your preparation as though about to hit across court but then turn the racket inside the ball with the wrist and play a drop shot. The opponent may not see it till after it has left the racket and will have to use up a lot of energy getting to the ball.

Wrong is Right for Forehand

Another important difference between the backhand and forehand is when you are retrieving a deep ball into the corner. On the forehand I really recommend you go into it with your right foot – in other words the 'wrong' foot – because then you can use your wrist to bring the ball across court if you want to (photos 15 and 16). If you go into the forehand corner with the left foot and try to flick the ball across court you will hit the ball into yourself. You can only hit down the wall.

On the backhand you must go in on the correct foot (which is the right foot) – photo 17 – but as the body is not so much in the way you can usually change the direction of your shot without problem. You must, though, go in on the correct foot. You cannot, as with the forehand, play a cross-court drop shot off the wrong foot from behind the body. The arm would be impeded and move into an absurdly stiff position. On the forehand the arm can bend. On the backhand it can't. Furthermore, the wrist can break inwards better (as on the forehand) than it can outwards. All this may be obvious if you study anatomy, but it is not so obvious to many squash players.

It is the backhand that so often leads to the dangerously big swipe from beginners, usually

15. Forehand retrieve down wall – impact (above left) Right foot forward will enable a quick movement to the shot and a quicker recovery to the T. It will also give room to hit cross-court ball. Wrist bent compensates for a late take. Open racket face gives height to ball

16. Forehand retrieve seen from front (above right) Note length of stride and how low the racket is. This shot is only to be recommended from a deep position

17. Backhand retrieve seen from behind (left) The angle of the shoulders is pointing towards the corner of the court and the back is completely turned on the front wall

18. Illegal swing (below left) A follow-through of this length is against the rules and dangerous to the opponent

19. Correct swing (below right) After pressing on to the ball at impact, the racket has a limited follow-through, across the body and upwards. Compare this with the illegal swing

20. Backhand drive – preparation Unlike forehand drive, the elbow is down. Wrist is slightly cocked. Shoulders half turned to the front wall. Eyes look over the shoulder

21. Backhand drive – impact Impact is around knee height. Head down

23. Backhand drive down wall – impact Impact is at about knee height, slightly in front of right knee

23a. Backhand drive, straight Impact point is just in front of the right leg

22. Backhand drive – follow-through Compare with photo 21. A longer follow-through is acceptable sometimes if the opponent is well clear

because they feel they have less power on this wing. In these situations it is all the more important to remember to press the racket on to the ball and to aim for the target. Don't aim for the back corner. The arm has to be relaxed. If it is stiff it will not spring back at the end of the follow-through; the swing will become excessive (photo 18). Compare with photo 19, the correct swing.

What many beginners do is to stiffen their arm and try to whack the ball as hard as they can. The results can be dreadful. They swing right round in a semi-circle (which is illegal) and risk hitting the opponent in the face. Instead, imagine holding a piece of string with a stone on the end. If you throw the stone it goes straight; then when you pull it back, the string bends in the way that the arm should.

If you feel like trying a big swipe on the backhand, remember the basics, and look at them in pictures 20, 21 and 22. Cock the wrist as you take your arm up. Prepare high and early. Turn the shoulders away from the ball and then make sure you swivel the body into the shot. Ensure you are making contact at the right place (see photo 23):

24. Backhand drive cross court – impact Impact is well in front of body, with the racket face at an angle to the front wall

24a. Backhand cross court Impact point slightly further in front of the leg. Compare racket angle with photo 23a

with the backhand it is just out in front of the right foot (see photo 23a). With the forehand it is level with the middle of the body. When hitting cross court, however, impact points are further forward (compare photo 23 with 24, and photo 25 with 26). Remember to press (photo 27). Compare also 23 with 23a and 24 with 24a.

Importance of the 'T'

The beginner should restrict himself to learning basic drives down the wall and cross court on backhand (photos 23 and 24) and forehand and then just a couple of other shots, the volley and the boast – that's all. The drop shot comes later. Many

25. Forehand down the wall – impact (left) Impact is immediately opposite the body, a few inches further back than the backhand down the wall shot
26. Forehand cross court – impact (below left) Impact is in front of left knee. Compare with forehand down the wall
27. Backhand drive – impact (below right) Shown from above, this picture helps show the pressing motion needed at impact

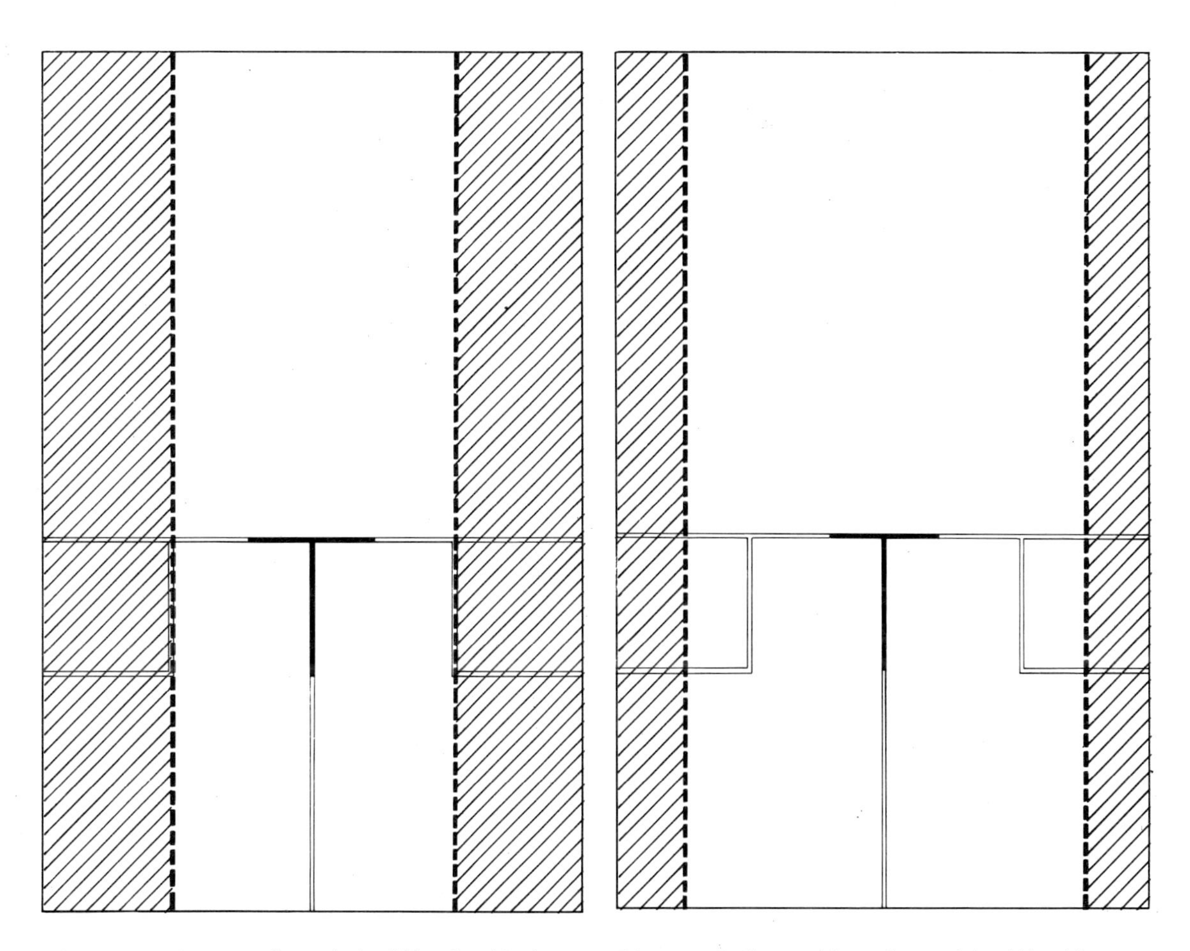

Diagram 2. The game of squash should be played in the shaded areas between the side wall and an imaginary dotted line extended from the side of each service box

Diagram 3. Players with good control should be able to play most of their squash in the shaded areas

rallies hang just on these basic drives to a length. Practise a good length all the time. Having done this it is necessary to understand the importance of taking up position on the T.

A squash court is not really very big, but it may seem so when you are out of position. It will come as a surprise to a beginner to be standing in one corner with the ball in the other and to find himself struggling. It is a simple but crucial tactic, therefore, to keep playing the ball to a length to the corners.

Imagine a line extending from the side of the service box to both back wall and front wall (see diagram 2). The game of squash should be played in the area between the dotted line and the side wall. Players with good control imagine the dotted line halfway across the service box, so that they are playing inside two-and-a-half feet (see diagram 3).

That leaves the centre part of the court. In the middle of that, at the junction of the rod lines, is the T. That is the best place for the non-striker to occupy during the rallies because it keeps you closest to all four corners (see diagram 4). It enables you to cut off any ball passing through the centre, either at front or back. Occupying the T position is vitally important for players of all standards. Top players reach the ball early by being aware of what their opponent is going to do. Beginners are not so aware and have trouble even getting to the ball if they are not on the T. In this strategically desirable position, even an unexpected shot should be within their reach in two or three strides. Always try to occupy the T, alert, ready and waiting, without letting the head of the racket droop (see photo 28).

Diagram 4. The T position is usually the best place for the non-striker to occupy because it enables him to cut off any ball passing through the centre of the court

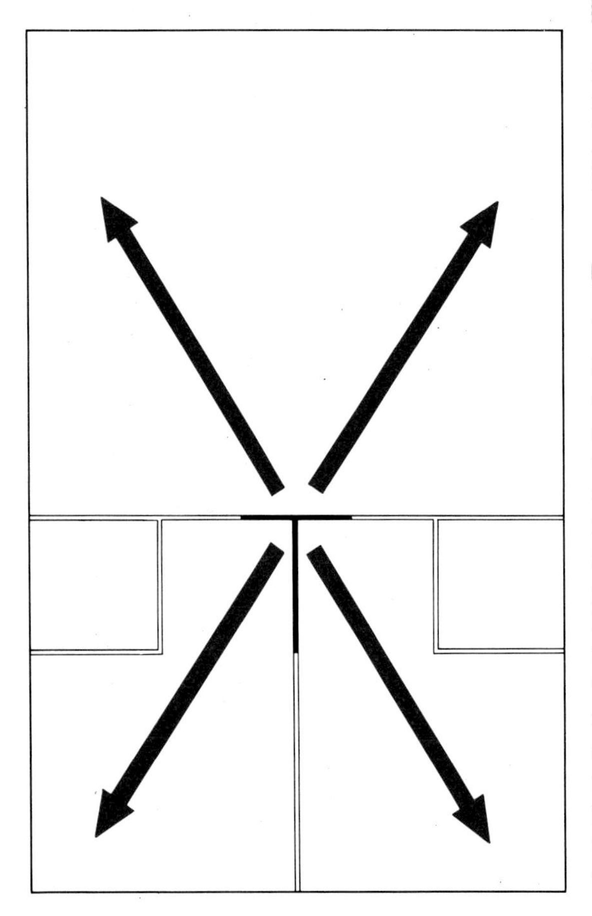

28. Ready position Head of the racket is up, head is forward. But weight is not too far forward on balls of the feet in case a movement backwards is necessary. In this particular picture the weight is slightly moving towards the backhand, as if to expect a cross-court shot into that corner

Volleying

It quickly becomes obvious that if a player stands on the T and the opponent plays through the middle of the court, a volley will be required. A volley, whether backhand or forehand, is similar to a drive in both preparation and production, though sometimes you may want to shorten the stroke a little (see photos 29 and 30). It should be practised carefully with a coach or a good feeder, hitting both straight and cross court. There are three heights to practise – at about knee height, waist height and above the shoulder. (Photos 33 and 34 show the backhand above shoulder height, down the wall and across court; 33a and 34a show the same shots at waist height. Photo 33b shows the very high backhand volley down the wall.) Develop the practices as before, close to the front wall to begin with, gradually moving back.

29. Forehand volley kill – preparation Eyes riveted on ball! Weight moving forward. Short backswing from wrist and elbow

30. Forehand volley kill – impact Wrist now firm. Weight forward

30a. Forehand waist high volley into the nick The elbow tucks into the body on impact

31. High forehand volley into the nick Hit slightly round the outside of the ball and ensure that the ball strikes the side wall before the floor. If it hits the nick, it rolls

The mid-court volley will be an attacking shot, but the one from the back is very important because this may be the first stroke that is required of you, when you have to return serve. If you are in front of your opponent it is often best to play the ball to the front of the court, perhaps trying to cut the ball into the nick (the place where floor and side wall join – photo 31). Another way of making your opponent move forward hurriedly is to volley the ball on to the side wall, whence it travels to the opposite front corner. (Whether played as a ground stroke or a volley this shot is called a boast.) It will need to be struck firmly. The ball loses pace after impact with the side wall (photo 32).

32. Backhand volley boast (far left) Note the racket face is open and the ball struck slightly upwards
33. Backhand volley down wall (centre) A good place to intercept on the volley is half court, in this case near the service box before the ball strikes the side wall
33a. Backhand waist high volley, straight (left) Note perfect balance. The ball should return to bounce at the back of the service box. The shot, taken early, will apply pressure on an opponent who has slightly overhit the ball

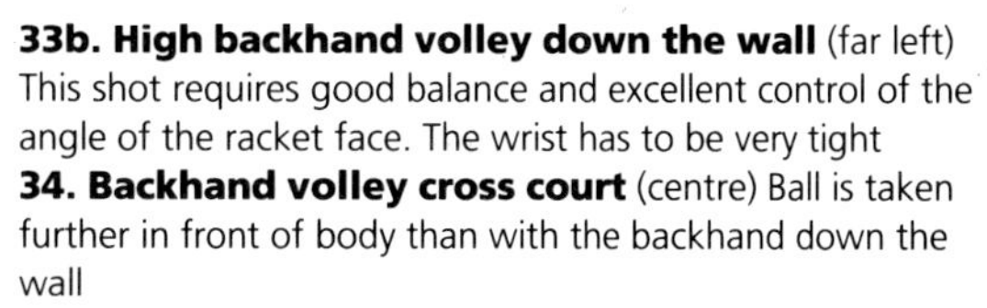

33b. High backhand volley down the wall (far left) This shot requires good balance and excellent control of the angle of the racket face. The wrist has to be very tight
34. Backhand volley cross court (centre) Ball is taken further in front of body than with the backhand down the wall
34a. Backhand waist high volley, cross court (left) A very early take to apply pressure to the opponent. The ball is driven hard to the opposite back corner, keeping possession of the T for the volleyer

When you are doing your volley practices down the wall, you should sometimes attempt a kill. Photos 29 and 30 show a kill being attempted and photo 30a shows a forehand volley into the nick. Note how the arm tucks into the body. Once you get back behind the short line you forget about killing the ball. Return it to the back corner instead. When you have retreated to beyond the short line that is the best practice for return of service, which can be played either cross court or down the wall (see photos 33 and 34).

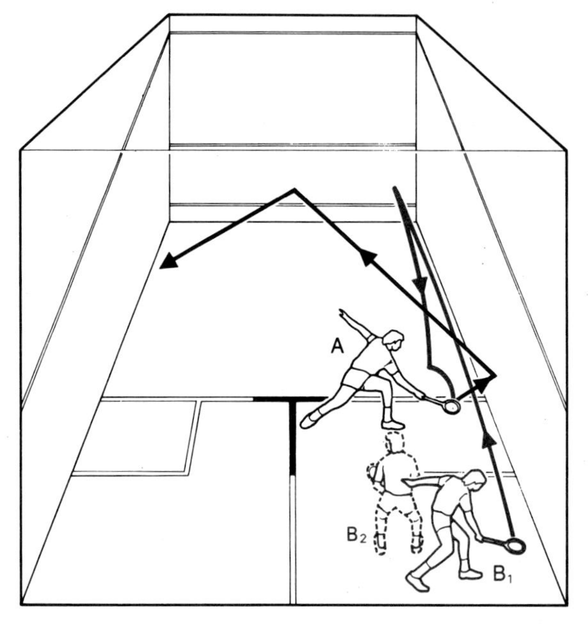

Diagram 5. (Above) Short length hit by player B enables player A to step in early and boast the ball into the side wall in front of his opponent, putting him in trouble. B must not move in front of A to go towards the T for fear of obstructing his view of the ball and giving away a penalty point

Cross Court or Down the Wall

The shot down the wall will often be safer than the shot played across court, provided you can send it close to the wall, or make it cling. With practice you should be able to do this. Play it short, though, and you will be in trouble, down the wall or not. The opponent will be able to step in and boast a short ball off the side wall, leaving you in a difficult position (see diagram 5). Good line and length will always make the straight shot a safe one, but you need to make sure you achieve both of these requirements.

Whether you should more often hit straight or across court depends on how well you play these strokes. At different times you should use both. Sometimes your opponent will not be on the T. He may have anticipated that you are going to hit down the wall, and have moved across to cut it off. If you can then hit high across court he will be in trouble, because the ball will go past him and drop in the back corner (see diagram 5a).

However, a cross-court at the wrong time can lose you the point immediately. Then an opponent has the chance to cut it off on the volley into the opposite front corner (see diagram 5b). The cross-

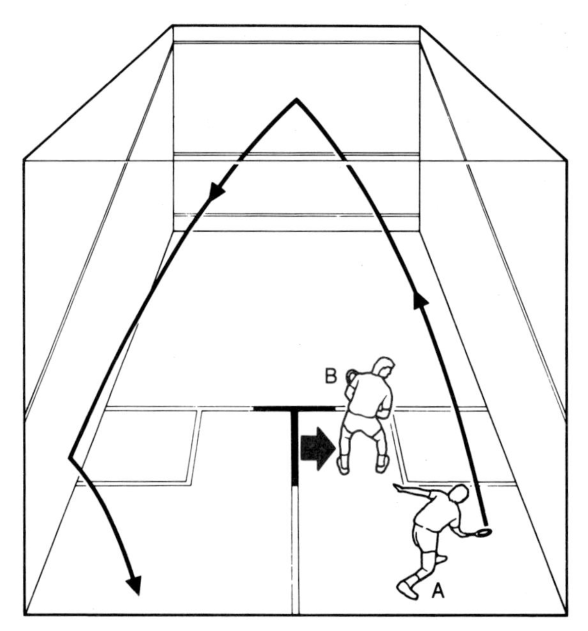

Diagram 5a. (Right) When B looks to make an intercepting attacking boast, as in diagram 5, that is the time to play a high cross-court shot. Normally this might be risky, but if B moves too soon the cross-court can be a winner, or near-winner

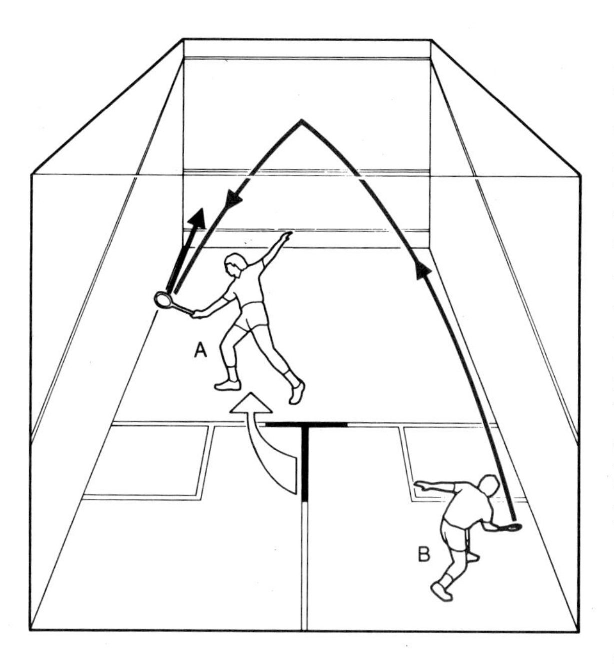

Diagram 5b. When a high cross-court shot is attempted with the opponent A in a good position on the T, B is likely to see the ball cut off on the volley into the front part of the court

court is a good shot when the opponent has edged towards the front. The secret is choosing the right shot for the right situation, and to learn that takes time. Every shot has to be played against the opponent's position, as in a game of chess.

The Boast

You can play this physical chess with a very few pieces – just the basic drive, forehand and backhand, the basic volley, and the boast. The drop shot, though important, should be learnt later. It is a more advanced shot and it is essential first of all to develop the basics. These create the situations in which the drop shot can be played. We can instead learn the boast at this stage and that will perform a similar function in taking the ball to the front of the court. The attacking boast, as you can see from photo 35 of the forehand and 36 and 37 of the backhand is played from a position where you are in front of your opponent (see diagram 5). It is played pretty well facing the side wall, although when trying a disguise you may not always do this. The defensive boast, by contrast, is played with the back turned on the back wall and from a position behind the opponent. Photos 38 and 39 show the backhand from behind and above, at impact point. Photos 40 and 41 show the forehand preparation from above and the impact point from in front. With photo 40 note how the arm gets above the shoulder – the defensive boast will have to be hit hard to ensure it does not go into the tin. With practice, however, you can turn it into attack, with

35. Forehand attacking boast Played from far further up the court, this shot will take the opponent from the back to the front. The ball is hit only slightly upwards. Compare racket angle with the defensive boast, photo 41

36. Backhand attacking boast preparation Similar to trickle boast preparation, photo 37. Elbow down, head of racket up. With this shot, back is half turned to the front wall

37. Backhand attacking boast – impact Racket is turned inside ball, hitting most of the side, a little of the back, and a little underneath

a three-wall boast that lands in, or near, the nick (see diagram 6). It is the second bounce of the attacking boast that goes near the nick (diagram 7).

To learn the boast, stand in the front corner in the same position as you started learning the forehand drive. Hit part side and part back of the ball, and slightly underneath it, and hit from the forehand front corner on to the side wall. From there the ball travels to the front wall. Played close to the front in this way the shot is sometimes known as a trickle boast. This can send the opponent the wrong way (see photos 42 and 43 of backhand trickle boast, and photo 44 showing the shot from behind).

While you are practising the trickle boast on the forehand you will be able to feed yourself by returning a little backhand on to the front wall, round to the side wall and on to your forehand again (see diagram 8. Diagram 9 shows how this sends the opponent the wrong way). Do that twenty times and then, as before, try from further back. This time as you move further away, go towards the T. By the time you are playing these two shots from the T you will be developing a backhand cross-court towards the nick, as well as the boast. Make sure you do the same thing in the backhand front corner, once again moving back diagonally towards the T. Practise volleys in the same way. Hit a forehand volley boast followed by a cross-court volley and repeat the pattern, moving back towards the T as you become more successful. This is not so easy. A beginner will no longer be a beginner once he can do this.

How to Move

It will help you to think about how you move. This is not so obvious as it seems. Each person has his own individual way of standing or running and the

38. Backhand defensive boast from behind Ball is hit sharply upwards. Note open racket face. Go for a boast into the nick if you can, which will turn defence into attack. And yes, you can, if you practise for it!

39. Backhand defensive boast from above Ball is hit between the side wall and the right foot, and the back is turned on the front wall

40. Forehand defensive boast – preparation Notice how high the racket goes up. The ball will need to be struck hard, and the back is almost completely turned to the side wall

41. Forehand defensive boast – impact Contrast footwork with photo 16. Left leg is well across. Ball is hit well up

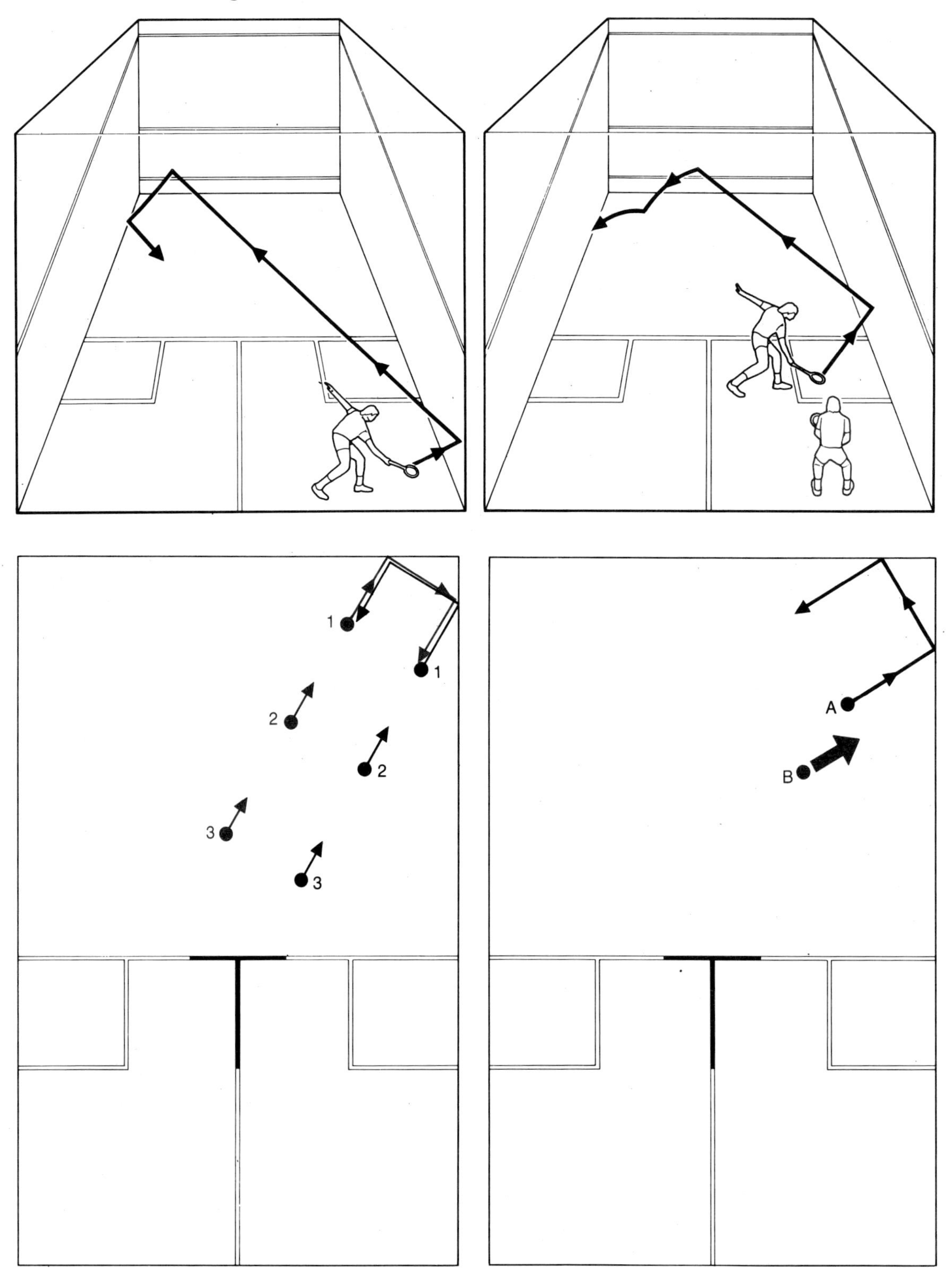
1
1
2
2
3
3
A
B

42. Trickle boast preparation Racket is cocked so that the ball could be struck in any direction. Intentions are not telegraphed by any movement of the body

43. Trickle boast – impact The head looks at the front wall and the opponent thinks a shot down the wall may be coming. But the racket is turned inside the ball, which is played on to the side wall

44. Trickle boast seen from behind The position of the head, facing towards the front wall, will encourage the opponent to think the ball is being hit straight. Instead it is trickled on to the side wall

Diagram 6. (Above left) The three wall boast is hit hard and low from the forehand back corner to strike the side, front and backhand side walls. As it contacts the third wall it should be close to or into the nick (junction of wall and floor) and may roll dead

Diagram 7. (Above right) A forehand boast from a more attacking position is aimed so that the second bounce is in or near the nick. The opponent only has a short space and time, just after the first bounce, in which to play an unhampered shot

Diagram 8. (Below left) Forehand trickle boast, returned by a backhand drop shot, and played from three different distances. This exercise can be performed by one person, moving gradually backwards towards the T

Diagram 9. (Below right) The trickle boast, played on to the side wall, encourages B to move in the same direction, but then leaves him with the opponent A between him and ball. Provided he had gone the wrong way he is then obliged to move round the opponent

best movement is the one that takes least out of you. There are jumps, hops, lunges, steps, and chassé movements. Much of the time, especially as you become a better player, you will not run. Whatever movement you choose to make it is important not to perform unnecessary gymnastics to get the ball. Recovery back to the T is just as important as actually reaching the ball.

Ideally you should always move comfortably, but if you find yourself short of time, then you have to decide quickly what is most expedient. This will depend on where you are standing, on anticipation and on ability to read your opponent's stroke. For this reason it is essential when you are on the T that you watch the ball wherever it goes. Simple as it sounds, many good players forget this golden rule in the heat of the moment.

When you are on the T, the first kind of movement is a series of little jumps. This is something you do rapidly and perhaps instinctively as the opponent prepares to strike the ball. These movements keep you balanced and ready for take-off. Wait flat-footed and it will take longer to get into action. The little jump is the perfect preparation for launching into a bigger jump, or a long step, or even a lunge.

The next movement depends on how close you are to the ball. Sometimes you will take a short step followed by a long one, sometimes *vice versa*. The important thing is that, as you reach the ball, you are not stretching too much. Quick recovery is all-important because that is how to apply more pressure. If you are always quickly back to the T again and hunting the ball, the opponent will become worried about how to keep it away from you. Gradually you can pressure him into error.

It is better therefore that with the last step before hitting the ball you are bending comfortably so there is a greater choice of what to do. Those slightly bent knees should be ready and able to press and jump back. The medium long movement is probably the best for a beginner. Two of these movements from the T will cover vast areas of the court, yet permit a comfortable recovery. If the ball goes into the corner it is better not to turn and run but to chassé to the ball. Do that by drawing one foot up to the other, before taking the other onwards in a sideways direction. You will save time and stay well-balanced but may have to play the ball off the wrong foot. You should nevertheless be able to recover from it quite well (see diagram 10).

Diagram 10. It is often better to chassé, rather than turn and run, particularly moving to the forehand corner. The right foot (in black) moves sideways three times and each time the left foot (in red) is drawn up alongside it to provide the push for further movement

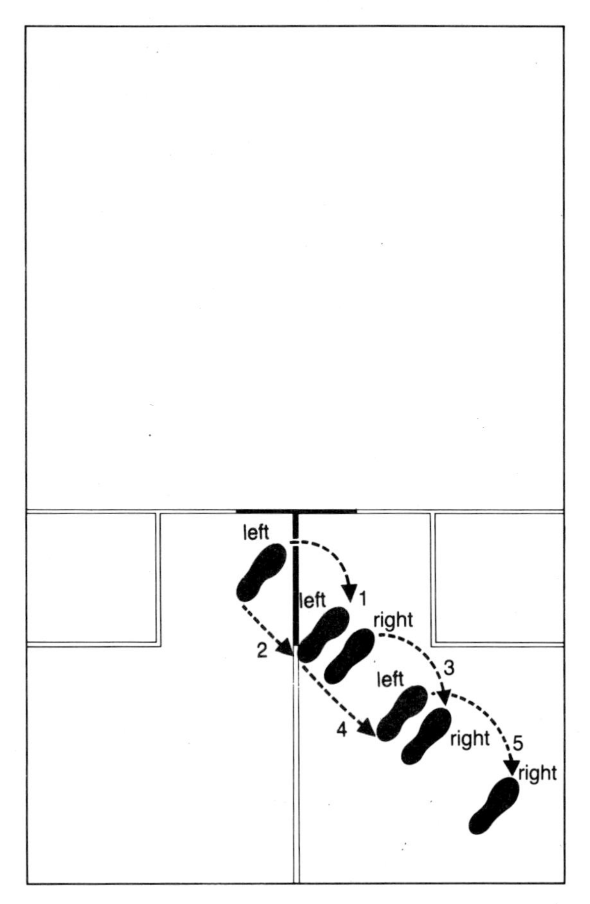

How to Watch

By now it must be clear that squash demands you keep tremendously alert. The player who anticipates what is about to happen and moves early, saves energy. Learning to read the little signs and clues about what your opponent is going to do requires practice, experience and concentration.

Always watch carefully. Whenever the opponent hits the ball, rivet your eyes on the ball and the racket. When the ball goes behind you, particularly when you are on the T, it is absolutely essential for you to turn your head to look. Never, never, never gaze at the front wall. If you do so, you risk losing the rally immediately. A boast can leave you for dead.

A lot of players still make this mistake, even if only for short periods when their concentration wavers or they grow tired. I have actually seen top players do this on return of serve. I don't know why. Is it because when they are losing they don't want to see the expression in the opponent's eyes?

To be serious, nobody should ever look at walls, opponent or anything other than the ball. It is not necessary that you should turn your whole body when the ball goes to the back. It is best for the body to be facing the front wall – then you can easily go to any of the four corners. Just turn your head. That one little thing can make the difference between winning and losing.

KHAN'S CONQUESTS III

JAHANGIR KHAN BEATS JANSHER KHAN:
9-6, 9-2, 9-2;
WORLD OPEN FINAL, AMSTERDAM 1988

This was the final some said I could not win. Jansher had beaten me nine times out of ten in previous matches. His ability to retrieve, his youth, fitness and stamina had constantly got him out of trouble and even enabled him to recover from two games down to beat me in Zurich and Monte Carlo. He had been enjoying an exceptional run and there were those who thought he would remain world number one for a long time.

Jansher was also the defending world champion. But I knew he could be beaten. For one thing I knew I had the ability to move him around more than he did me. I could volley better and play the ball short more consistently, to make him work during the long rallies. Sure, his capacity for covering the court was outstanding. I could expect few easy rallies. But if I could stay with him without being negative and without making mistakes, I knew I could get into a position to win the match. It would then be a question as to whether I had enough left to take it.

But first I had to build that position. That was a long job. The first rally made clear just how much work this could involve. It was a rally so unusual that people still remember and talk about it. It lasted nearly seven minutes, took more than 220 shots, and proved that a battle of wills would help decide the match, as well as of skills or fitness.

It ended with Jansher hitting the ball out of court. I had made a point as well as won one. There would be nothing easy for him. Now I had to make another. He would have to work to win all his points. Many phases of the early rallies were up and down the walls, but if there was a chance to play a straight drop or cut the ball off on the volley I would not hesitate to do so, to apply more pressure.

There were few of these to begin with. It took fifteen minutes to get to 2-1, and twenty to reach 3-1. Then I got ahead 6-2 after my lob landed perfectly in a back corner. But he got back to 6-6 and still the rallies were very long. It became increasingly clear that it was vital to win the opening game if I was to have a real chance of winning the match.

Then I got an unexpected break – a high backhand volley from Jansher that hit the tin and got me to 7-6. It was followed by what I thought were opportunities for playing short and, sure enough, by trying a backhand drop from deep and then a sudden boast, I got the game 9-6. But it had taken 40 minutes and cost plenty of energy.

Early in the second game there was an incident which significantly altered the mood. I was certain that a drive to the back had touched Jansher as it had come through, and yet the referee awarded only a let. I felt it should have been a point and I went out of the door to say so. The referee disagreed.

Had Jansher thought so? Whatever was in his mind Jansher's concentration seemed affected because in a short time he made three mistakes. I was still making very few, and was also playing well defensively, which pleased me. That had not always been the case in my recent matches.

This enabled me to keep the pressure going through the second game which, though shorter, was still 25 minutes long. I was feeling the effort I had made. At the same time I felt I was gradually getting into a position from which the match could be won.

I was right. In the third game I got quickly to 3-0. This was roughly the situation in which I had been in Monte Carlo only a month before, when I had

lost. I grew tense and made a couple of mistakes. I could not afford more of that. I had built the platform but had to time the jump for victory right.

Two strokes, both reverse angles, helped me do that. I had hardly used this stroke at all before. Yet now when I had a mid-court opening I suddenly swung a forehand across my body and on to the backhand side wall to see it die as it whipped back across to the other wall. It was 4-2. Jansher was surprised.

A few moments later I produced another and Jansher did not get to that one either. They seemed to finish him. He was 7-2 down and never looked like making the long drawn-out recovery of which everyone knew he was capable.

Maybe those many long rallies had drained something from him. He had had to absorb more pressure than before. At any rate he did not get to the shot I played on match point either. And, in a finish that came quickly and was a great relief, I was world champion again.

It was a turning point. Jansher did beat me from time to time after that, but never with the same regularity. I managed to create the feeling that whenever I really needed to beat him there was a good chance of doing so. But the timing of those two reverse angles I shall always remember.

Lesson Build a platform before you jump.

CHAPTER 4

IMPROVING

Most of what has been said so far has been relevant to defensive play – control, good length, good line, preparation, practice, and a little about where to put the ball. Why do we learn the defensive game first? To create the opportunity of getting into positions to kill the ball. The basis of squash is to keep the opponent at the back of the court, or to move him to the four corners and to force him to give a weak return. Then you attempt attacking shots. That's what we'll deal with here.

I'm against people going on court and playing game after game without learning the right way to play. It will help nobody unless you set out on a proper programme of learning. It is natural for a player to want to play games as soon as possible. But you can have little competitions with yourself as you go along. It is not a good idea for a beginner to jump in at the deep end.

By now we have reached a level appropriate for a good player who has acquired many of the basics, or perhaps for a promising junior. But before learning to finish a rally it is important to know how to get into position to do it. Usually this will be from in front of your opponent. That means you will be, or will have been, on the T, or close to it. If the opponent is in front of you, then kill the ball at the back of the court by hitting a length. If he is behind, kill the ball with a drop shot to the front, or with a boast drop shot, or an attacking boast.

The Drop Shot

The drop shot is probably the most important of these shots. It can often finish the rally or, if it has been played tight on the side wall, it can set things up for the hard kill next time. Many people are afraid to use it in case they put the ball into the tin. You can rid yourself of that fear by throwing the ball to yourself, and then hitting it deliberately into the tin, gradually hitting it higher till you are striking on to the wall. This helps eliminate negative reaction or nervous anticipation about the ball striking the tin.

Another aid to steadiness is to play the drop shot with more cut. The ball will then stay on the racket face longer, which helps control and reduces mistakes. It will cause the ball to come down more sharply from the front wall, making the drop shot fall shorter. It may also turn the ball towards the side wall more. It is a simple shot, similar to playing to a length, but contact is made, not very hard, near the bottom of the ball and there is less follow-through. Make sure your balance is good.

Although you don't need to take your racket back a long way for a drop shot, it is often good to do so for purposes of deception (photo 45 on the forehand and 48 on the backhand). Take the arm and racket above your head as though for a drive, although as it comes down it won't be travelling with the same power and speed. When it descends to the level of your armpit you will bring your arm in and stop it slightly (photo 46 forehand, 49 backhand). A little jerk will come into the shot, and the follow-through will be more of a push (photo 47 forehand, 50 backhand). Compare 46 with 51, showing the target of the nick.

45. Forehand drop shot preparation High racket preparation indistinguishable from forehand drive or kill

46. Forehand drop shot – impact The ball is taken late, thus increasing the likelihood of the opponent committing himself. It will be aimed to travel slightly upwards to just above the tin, and to land in the nick

47. Forehand drop shot – follow-through Short follow-through. Eyes on the ball

48. Backhand drop preparation As with the preparation for the trickle boast, the ball could be struck anywhere from this position

49. Backhand drop – impact The ball is contacted low. The head and hand are both steady

50. Backhand drop – follow-through The ball has been played straight and the follow-through is short

51. Forehand drop shot – impact Compare with photo 40: low impact, steady head, the ball nicks and rolls

52. Body masking hand and wrist A clever player will mask his intentions like this from a variety of situations

Disguise

It is a fairly simple thing to disguise the drop shot, and a number of others as well, with your body, especially if your opponent is behind you. Qamar Zaman has been a master of this. I myself drop the racket head to do it – so that the racket, arm, and wrist are all hidden by the body (see photo 52) – and use a little flick of the wrist to change the direction. This can also be done with the trickle boast, sending the opponent the wrong way (see photo 42 and 43 and diagram 8).

You can play the drop shot several ways. If the ball is low and you have enough time, then 'get right down to it' as the text books say (see photos 46 and 49). If it is bouncing high, let the ball come down again to the level of your knee. Then you can cut underneath it and also be in position to perform many different strokes.

If you hit the ball when it is high, from the top, you can't do much with it. All you can do is to press the ball down. If the wrist is a little bit loose or you angle it wrongly, the ball could easily go into the tin. Hitting from underneath lessens the likelihood of putting the ball down, and it increases the number of things you can do with the same preparation – facilitating further disguise.

You can play the backhand drop shot more easily from in front of your body than the forehand and therefore probably from a wider range of positions (see photos 48, 49 and 50). You can mask it more easily too than the forehand (photo 52). If you want to mask it with your body, you have to compensate with your wrist. But you are behind the ball on the forehand, and the weight behind it sometimes gives more control. With the backhand there's less body push; it's mostly arm.

How to Practise Drops

When you practise the drop shot it is usually best to start from the forehand front corner. Then move further down the forehand side wall right to the back (see diagram 11). A coach can be of great value in feeding the ball for this particular type of practice, but you can do it for yourself, throwing the ball on to the front wall with your hand.

People may question why you should play a drop shot right from the back, but a lot of good players use it from this position. Done correctly, it is a winner. That is because it has an element of surprise, especially off the back wall when the normal reply is to hit a length. Even if it is not a winner, a forehand drop played straight is still dangerous if it comes back close to the wall, and clings.

Another excellent practice idea is to gradually move back from the forehand front court, as before, but only to the short line. From there, continue hitting drops while moving along the short line, playing the forehand drop from a wider and wider angle (see diagram 12). As you move

Diagram 11. Precise forehand drop shots from different positions, moving backwards – even from the back part of the court

Diagram 12. After practising forehand drop shots moving back from the front corner to the short line, then move along the cut line at a wider and wider angle towards the T, trying to put the ball into the nick

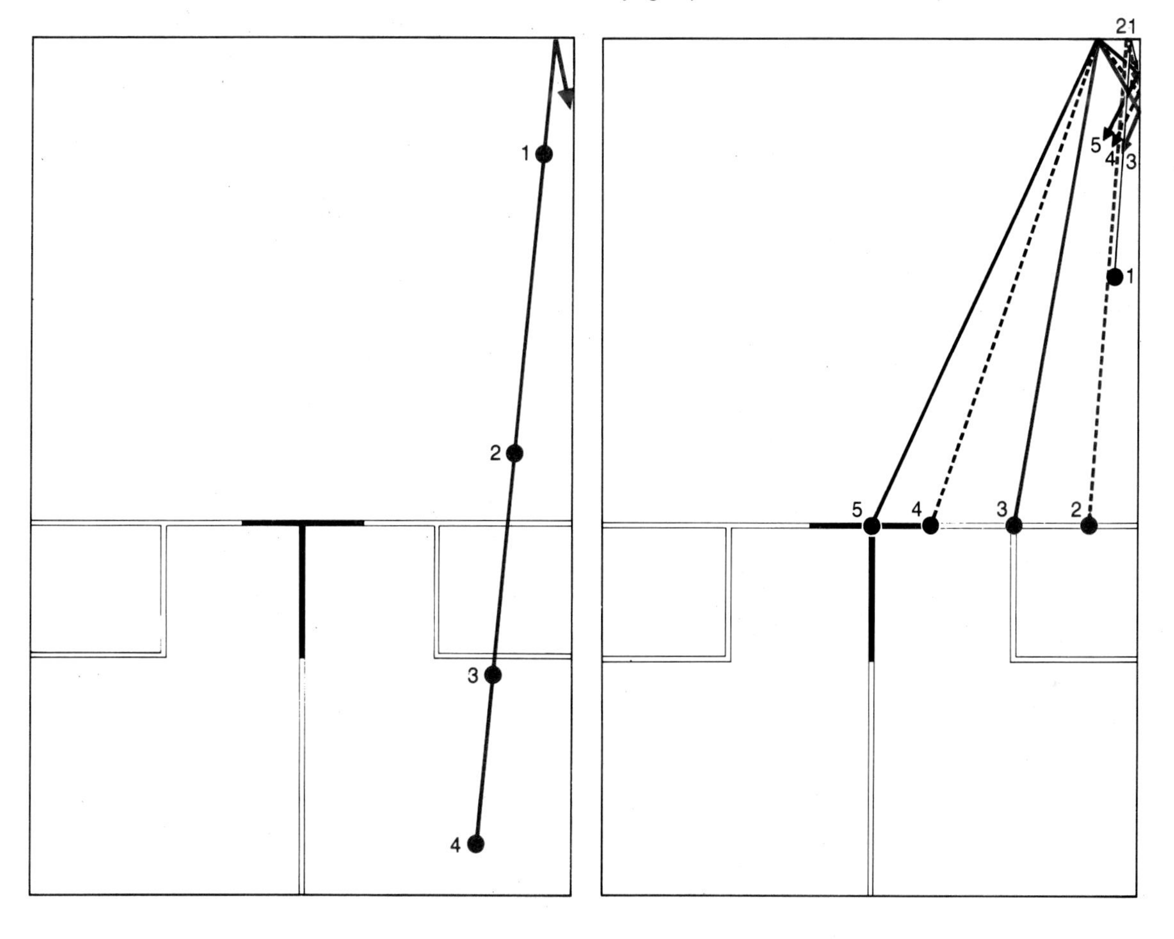

towards the T you will get into a wide enough position to try to hit a nick (the join between the floor and the wall). Even if you can't do it, try to make sure the shot hits the side wall before it hits the floor: then it will stay down low and short. That will be the next best thing to a nick. If it hits the floor first it will sit up (see diagram 13).

It is necessary to practise from all areas of the court. So keep right along the short line to the backhand wall – throw the ball, drop shot, throw the ball, drop shot – still playing the forehand drop. Keeping it low on to the front wall is most important to make sure of a nick and shallow angle. There won't be that many situations in which you will want to play this shot. You'd rather play the backhand from that position. But if you do this, you can turn and face the side wall and then make the same shot.

With the backhand drop shot you should attempt the same thing moving along the short line towards the T, playing towards the backhand wall. When you are hitting the backhand drop shot straight you must try to make it cling. You cannot hit a nick from a length but you can make it stay on the wall. A little slice may make it cling once it touches.

Diagram 13. If the drop shot played cross court strikes the side wall or the nick first (see A), it will come back close to whence it came. If it strikes the floor first (see B) it will travel further down the court

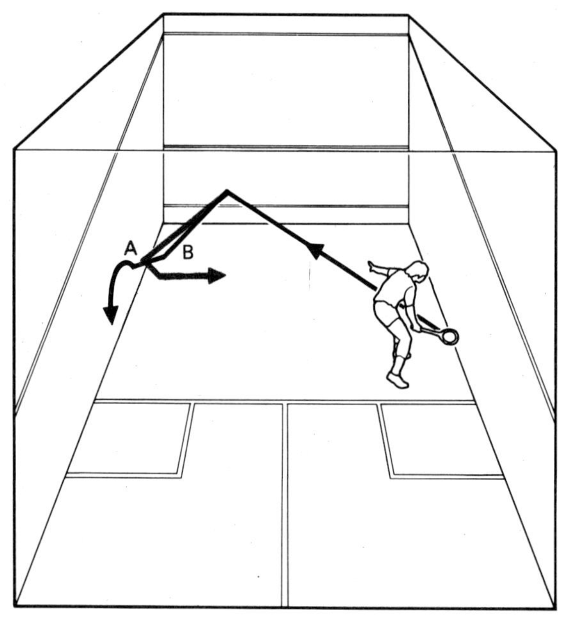

Beginners can learn to play down the wall from some way out into the middle of the court. The better the player, the closer to the side wall he will be able to practise. Eventually it should be possible to play within an inch or two of the wall every time. The same will apply to hitting the nick. First you will strike the side wall a foot or two up, and gradually you get it to bounce lower, nearer to the join of the floor and the wall.

Changing Sides

After playing backhands all along the short line till you get to the forehand side wall, you play a forehand cross-court drop, long distance, into the opposite front corner. Then the same on the other side, from the backhand side wall standing on the short line, play a cross-court backhand drop into the forehand front court. The routine is that you throw the ball up towards the front wall straight, so that it comes back down the side wall, but hit it cross-court. If you are hitting it right so that the ball hits the side wall in the opposite front corner before touching the floor, then you won't have to run to get the ball. It will come straight back to you. If it hits the floor first, you are in for a lot of fetching and carrying.

These are excellent exercises and worth practising regularly because a well-controlled drop shot from any part of the court is a tremendous asset. It will give you the ability to take your opponent to every part of the court and keep him guessing. After a while the ball may cool down during this exercise and you may have to hit it up and down the wall a few times to warm it.

Doing all the exercises with enthusiasm and with a good attitude is essential. Try not to hold the ball in your left hand (assuming you are right-handed). Use your racket to pick up the ball. If you make a mistake, don't stop the exercise, but try to make a correction with your racket. Feed yourself with your racket; that is another way of developing ball control. Never waste time. If the ball is going away from you, don't walk after it. Run, pick it up with your racket, come back into position and throw the ball again immediately. Go straight back into the routine.

The next step is practising with the ball in the air – using the volley drop. Do all the same things that you have just done, but at waist level. Throw the ball to the right height and try to kill it on the volley drop. The elbow comes into the waist a little as you make contact (photo 30a). Then do the same thing, with volley boasting, as with the boast drive. Make sure all shots are practised with both backhand and forehand from all the areas on the court, as before.

There are three heights at which you need to develop all the shots – knee height (drive), waist height (volley) and head height (overhead). Practise all of these. Practise for a good length as well, with a ball at the front, at the centre, and at the back. Go through all of the shots in all of these places. Then you will have covered every possibility.

53. Forehand kill preparation Compare with photo 9. Elbow up, as before. But the body is more erect

54. Forehand kill – follow-through The kill impact point is similar to the drive, but the follow-through is lower and a little slower

The Kill

Another important shot, once you have your opponent out of position, is the kill, the hard low kill. The player who has someone to feed him is especially fortunate where this exercise is concerned. If you have no feeder you should practise by throwing the ball up to yourself, but your progress will be slower. The ball does not come back to you.

Stand in the forehand corner, throw the ball and kill. Next time, throw the ball close to the side wall, but not so close that you cannot hit the ball in the middle of the racket. If it is *too* close, don't hit it. Avoid racket breakage! Do all the exercises as before. There isn't much difference in the production of the forehand kill and the forehand drive, except that because the target is a little lower when killing the ball the racket may come more from the top, pressing down. Look at the preparation and follow-through in photos 53 and 54. Don't actually close the racket over the ball. And don't put more wrist into this shot in order to hit it harder, unless the ball has gone slightly past you. Just hold the grip tight.

Power comes from the shoulder. Because the elbow is very relaxed, the jerk of the arm also gives power. The jerk from the elbow, which was originally bent, is like the throwing of a cricket ball: there is some wrist but mostly the power comes from the straightening of the elbow. After you've practised it well, do the same on the backhand.

The Lob

Another potential winner is the lob. If it is played from the back of the court it is used to slow the pace of the game down, but from the front it can be

55. Lob – impact moment Once again, intentions are disguised. Opponent has to look to see whether a drop, a drive or a lob is being played. The cross-court lob strikes high on the front wall

56. Lob – follow-through By the time the opponent has guessed that a lob is coming it is passing high over the cut line near the side wall. He has moved too late to cut it off on the volley

more aggressive. The opponent can be lured forward to cover the possible drop shot, only to find he is unable to cut off a ball passing over him to the back corner. The result is that he ends up very close to the back wall.

It is vital to hit the correct part of the ball. The racket travels underneath even more than it does with the drop shot. It is tilted back, very open, and has to travel very low. It must go right underneath the ball. You can put a little slice on a lob but more important is to strike the correct part of the ball. Many players do not understand this and continue to hit the back of the ball, especially on the lob serve. Also remember to hit high on the front wall, a foot or two below the out line (see photos 55 and 56). Some coaches say aim for five feet above the service line. This is wrong.

Do the same routine as before: down-the-wall lobs, then moving back and lobbing right from the back. Then practise the cross-courts. These cross-court lobs are the potential winners (see photos 57 and 58 for the backhand lob). If your opponent is on the T, then aim straight into the corner. When a lob bounces, the ball will not 'shoot' as with a shot hit to a length. The second bounce of a good length shot goes to the back wall nick. With the lob, the first bounce is close to the back wall, much closer than for a drive to a length.

Lob Service

The lob service should strike the side wall just short of the back wall and then roll close to that wall so that it is very difficult to hit. I have not so far said anything about serving. That is because I do not want to encourage beginners to play competitively before they are ready. They can and probably will, but I don't want to encourage it.

Ideally a service should kiss the side wall, rather

57. Backhand lob – impact moment The opponent is leaning slightly forwards, half expecting a drop shot. The lob is struck from a low, late position, maximizing disguise

58. Backhand lob – follow-through Once again, the ball strikes the front wall high and passes over the cut line before the opponent has moved very far from the T

than contact it hard. Therefore, it is better to serve from out in the middle of the court and not from near the side wall. From the right hand box, this can sometimes mean serving with the backhand. By putting slice on the ball, it can be made to turn towards the back wall.

Many players serve like this and because the opponent cannot return it become satisfied that it is a good service. That may not be so. The opponent may merely be a poor receiver. A test is necessary to make sure the serve is really as good as it should be.

Diagram 14. A service practice to test its accuracy: the ball should end up on the forehand side wall not more than two racket lengths from the back (red dotted line)

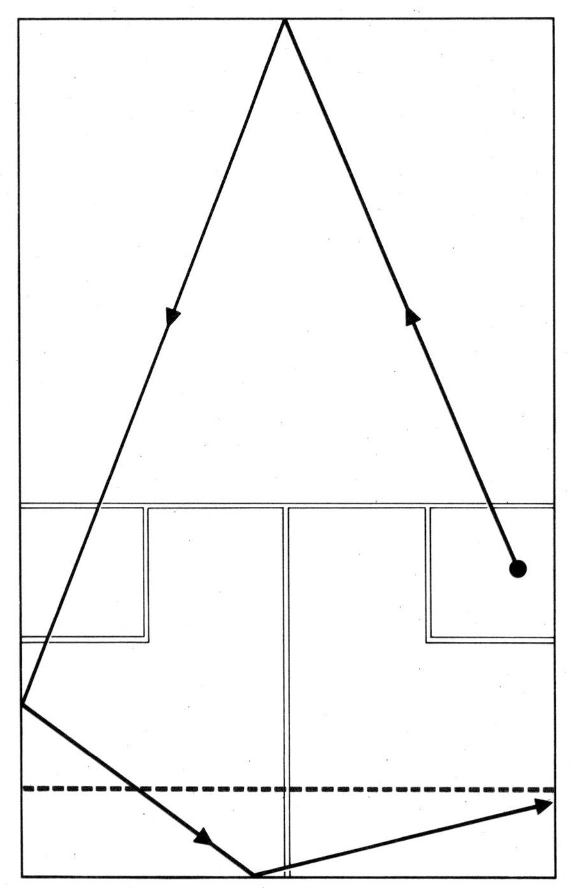

59. Forehand lob serve, left box The server is again in position quickly to get to the T. The ball contacts the front wall a few feet to the right of centre

Measure two lengths of the racket from the back wall upon the forehand side wall and mark the spot with a racket cover or anything you like. Then serve so that the ball strikes the backhand side wall, then the back wall and finally bounces along the back of the court. It should end up less than two racket-lengths from the back wall by the time it reaches the forehand side wall. You will have served as accurately as possible if you can do this (see diagram 14).

Service Tactics

There are almost no service aces at a high standard. The aim is usually to limit the angle so that the opponent cannot easily hit the front wall with his return. He may then have to play a defensive boast. This will not happen if the ball is served so that it comes into court at right angles off the

60. Backhand lob serve, right box This enables the server to come far closer to the T position whilst striking the ball

61. Forehand lob serve, right box The ball is struck above waist level and only a little below the out line. It connects with the side wall at the back of the service box, high up

back wall. If you do as I suggest, and the opponent stays in the backhand corner, the ball will pass behind him. Then he will be in trouble.

To gain sufficient room to take the racket back properly he will have to move, usually into the middle of the back wall. Sometimes there is not enough time, and a defensive boast off the backhand side wall results. If he turns right round and tries to boast it off the forehand side wall he is in real difficulties, and if he tries to boast it off the back wall, that is the weakest return of the lot.

Getting the angle of the serve right clearly matters a great deal. The forehand serve from the backhand box enables a player to move near to the middle of the court to get the best angle (photo 59). For similar reasons, some players try serving with the backhand from the forehand box (photo 60). But the forehand from the forehand box can give more spin and very often more control. That's the serve I favour from that side (see photo 61).

Though the high lob serve is a good delivery, it is still a sensible idea to vary the height and pace. A high backhand volley is a return that lesser players may find difficult, and even at a high level opponents are less likely to do much with. A good serve may create other possibilities.

Hammer Serve

For instance, sometimes the opponent anticipates a high serve and starts to move back because he feels he cannot cut the ball off early. This is the perfect time to serve hard and low, a hammer serve, which bounces into or near the nick at the back of the service box. That can sometimes cause a surprise (photos 62 and 63).

Players with bad habits sometimes receive serve by turning towards the side wall. They are expecting (in the backhand court) that it will always

62. Forehand hammer serve, left box The ball is struck only just above the service line and hard towards the nick at the back of the service box

63. Forehand hammer serve, right box This serve creates a wider angle and comes further out from the side wall after making contact with it

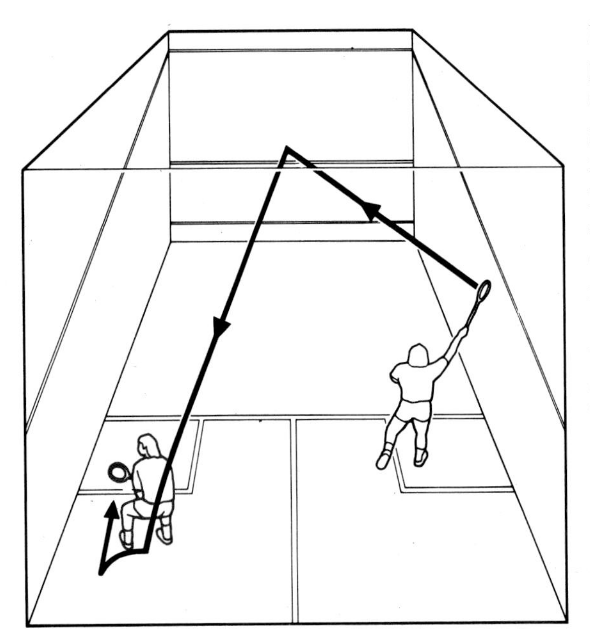

Diagram 15. A hammer serve aimed towards the right shoulder may catch out a receiver expecting the ball to come to him on the backhand. Even if he gets out of the way he may be in difficulties because of the awkward angle at which the ball came off the back wall

be served on to their backhand. When this happens, hit the serve hard towards the right shoulder (see diagram 15). I have sometimes managed to hit players on the body, even good players, that way. It is the quickest and easiest method of winning the point. Especially in the later stages of a match, the opponents may be too slow to get out of the way easily. Also, when he is tired, his eyes may not focus so well.

Sometimes the opponent will try to straighten up to allow the ball to pass behind him. Even if he does this, it can be awkward to take the ball off the back wall. Sometimes it may land close to a back wall nick. Occasionally he will find he has saved himself by moving forward only to discover that he is in further difficulties because the ball is coming at him again: he has moved into the line of it. This is what you are looking for in squash: the weak return rather than the service ace.

Movement After Serving

After any shot it is usually necessary to cover the T. You can then economically reach all four corners of the court. The serve is no exception. It is best to serve from very close to the short line. On the backhand side, put your right foot in the box, left foot out towards the middle, and take a medium-length step. By the time the ball is leaving the front wall you will be on the T and in the ready position. It hardly takes more than a single stride.

On the forehand side, again put the right foot in the service box, and the left foot out. With a forehand service, it requires a different movement to get to the centre because the T will not be facing the server. Use a chassis movement, drawing one leg up towards the other in a sideways direction. This may be a little slower, but because the forehand takes the body across towards the T naturally there may not be much difference in the speed of movement.

Return of Serve

The return of serve is best practised by the volley exercises described. Move back into the forehand quarter of the court and volley from the forehand side, down the wall and cross court; same on the backhand side. (Note the different racket angles in photos 33a and 34a.) If you have done these exercises it should not be difficult to return.

A decision has to be made whether to strike a good serve before or after it hits the side wall (see diagram 16). The volley boasting exercises suggested should help you to cope. The answer to the serve that presents difficulties for lesser players – the one that requires them to volley off the side wall – is to practise. Mistakes are often the result of being indecisive. It is better to take the ball early if you can, before it hits the wall, to try to seize the initiative. Look at the picture of the high backhand volley down the wall, photo 33b. It is crucial that you make up your mind or mistakes can be made, in the same way accidents on the road sometimes happen because of late decisions – drivers allow themselves to drift into two minds about overtaking.

I have seen such indecision even at a high level. I saw one leading player go for a high ball, start to play a volley drop and then get in two minds about it. He started and then thought he should play a length. In the end he did neither. The ball ended on the floor: it did not even reach the tin. It was

Diagram 16. Better to try to strike the return of serve in position one, before it hits the side wall, unless the ball is overhit. Position two requires a more difficult volley as the ball changes height and direction after contacting the wall

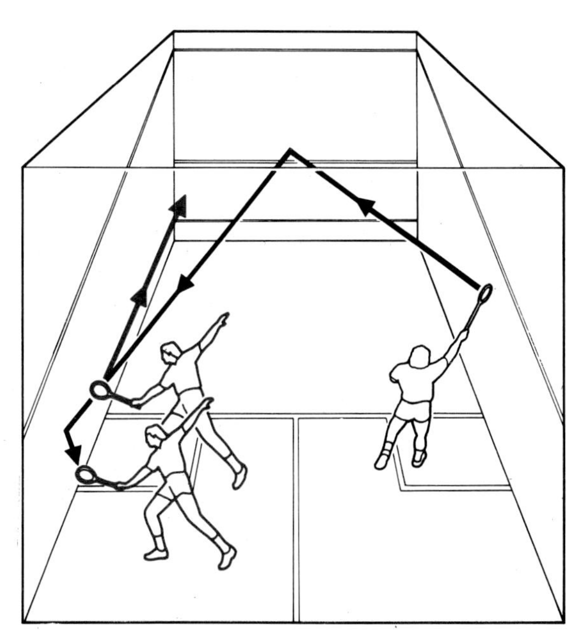

remarkable and quite instructive. What happened was that at the last moment he stopped his racket, and the ball hit his racket instead of *vice versa*. To return serve well you must be in a ready position, and you have to make up your mind. As your standard improves, and your confidence with it, so will your ability to make a decision.

Anyone who has completed the suggested exercises will now be good enough to play games or matches. The risk of bad habits should have been reduced. Competitive instincts will be kept alive by little competitions, seeing whether or not you can hit a shot twenty times or fifty times without mistake. Real competition, of course, will feel very different.

Pressure

Playing competitively for the first time creates pressure. That means pressure upon you as a person, testing whether or not you can perform the skills you have practised when it really matters. The outcome will in part depend on you yourself, your character and personality. Pressure makes some play worse, some better. It makes most of us perform differently. It is essential that you go on court determined to carry out what has been learned in practice. This will not be as easy as you think. Your attitude needs to be good. Sometimes players completely forget to hit a good length and to play patiently. They are tempted to try something extra, something that they cannot be sure they can do. Learn to recognize your capabilities.

Don't be too disappointed if the pressure of competition makes it harder for you to do things you thought you could. Pressure makes players change their minds, change their techniques; it even changes their physical make-up. It can make them feel tired when they are not. Adaptability is at a premium. Though you practise shots in a precise position, in a match it is never like that. Every situation is different.

Often it's a good idea to go back to the routines to recreate the pressures of competition, trying to repeat them under the pressure of movement. Start off with ball control exercises, having the ball fed to you, then produce the same shots moving to a position where you have to stretch. You will need someone feeding to do this. You can recreate some of the situations that occur in a match. Practise until you get tired. You may have to play a long match and still need to play the right shots.

Throughout all this you should learn something about yourself. You may learn when you lose your temper, when you get anxious, when you get tired, and you'll certainly learn when you feel like giving up. You must be prepared to discover weaknesses in yourself that you didn't know existed.

This is not always easy to accept. We must remember what may have ceased to be obvious – that we are all human beings. Why did you lose? There is more to be learnt there than anywhere. You practised and practised, and then suddenly in the match you made mistakes. What happened? If you can start to find answers to these questions you are on the way to becoming both a better squash player and a better person.

Jahangir and Hunt, who pressured each other to the limit and still went on

KHAN'S
CONQUESTS IV

JAHANGIR KHAN BEATS RODNEY MARTIN
9-2, 3-9, 9-5, 0-9, 9-2;
BRITISH OPEN FINAL, WEMBLEY 1989

I felt more tension in this final than in any other British Open. That was not just because it was the only one that went the full five games. It was also partly because there were disputed refereeing decisions at an important stage. This complicated the match, as I knew I could not allow free gifts to someone like Rodney Martin, probably the most dangerous attacking player of all. He might take too many points with his skill, without donations. He had beaten me before, and was capable of it again.

This too was a final I needed to win more than any before. Victory would give me a record equal to Geoff Hunt's eight titles – something I wanted to achieve ever since losing narrowly to Hunt in the 1981 final. Of course I believed I could win, but I had a feeling it might be tough. Sure enough there was a crisis during the fourth game when it seemed that my great ambition might be slipping away from me. For these reasons the whole contest was an exercise in handling pressure greater than any I had experienced before.

It all started well enough. I began with a high-paced attack, hoping to hurry him and deny him opportunities to make openings or winners. Mostly that was what happened, and I won the first game reasonably quickly, in 19 minutes.

Early in the second game Martin had a slice of luck when he rimmed the ball and produced a mishit winner that regained him the service. I gave him a rueful smile but was soon to feel very different.

Four winners from the middle of his racket followed, two from short, two from deep positions, and suddenly a door to his dangerous talent had been opened. I tried to lengthen the rallies and got back to 3-5 with a penalty point, but never regained the initiative. I also made one or two mistakes at the end of a game which he took 9-3. The good thing was that it had taken him 28 minutes and quite a lot of effort to do it.

The start of the third game was obviously important. I forced the pace up again. A determination to attack at speed helped me to dominate the early phases. I found the openings for two winners, he tried for two winners and missed, and I had a 4-0 lead. It was a valuable cushion.

I could not quite keep the pace of the exchanges as high throughout a 22-minute game but I was able to hang on to my advantage to take it 9-5. Some of the rallies brought long applause from the crowd, and there were some great retrieves from both of us, with the ball being moved from the back to the front and back again, as well as from side to side. The effort had taken something from both of us.

I thought I had made an important step towards victory. Even though I knew matches against world-class opponents are never over till the last point, I felt hopeful and slightly relieved to be 2-1 up. I could not possibly have guessed what was to happen.

The match suddenly swung away from me. A penalty point, a forehand into the nick from Martin, a tin from me, two no-let decisions against me and then another Martin winner got him to 4-0. After that I was refused another two lets, even though I felt I could not get past my opponent to the ball. I could not understand it at all.

I challenged the referee and then asked for the tournament referee. Some people later said that I was close to quitting, which was untrue. Instead I was determined to make my point now rather than later, when it might be too late. The tournament referee said that there was no need to change the match referee because I could win without it.

Of course I played on, but by then Martin had his tail up. He was playing some of his best squash and there were some mistakes from me too. He finished the fourth game off with a backhand volley drop shot winner. It was 9-0 to him and the crowd was roaring.

This was one of the most important moments of my career. There was now maximum pressure. I had to regain the initiative against the most dangerous opponent on the circuit, and I had to do it immediately. I must regain my concentration. I might feel like boiling over with annoyance but I had to turn my mind to ice.

I knew we had been playing for a long time (100 minutes as it turned out) and I thought he might tire. The fourth game may have appeared one-sided but it had not been such a short one. Changing the teleball each game can also help aggression a little bit because a new ball can be quicker off the front wall and through the air. This may have assisted me to summon up one more attack.

The outcome was spectacular. Within two minutes I had a five-point lead. He could not answer it. I had a look at him and I could tell from his expression that he was struggling. I knew now that if I kept it going I would win. But I did not expect that I would break him down so quickly. In five minutes I had pushed through to a victory I shall never forget. Only a short time earlier I had been in danger of defeat. Resolve and concentration had turned disaster into triumph.

Lesson Under pressure, close your mind off. Practise relaxed concentration.

CHAPTER 5

PRACTISING

I can now reveal my on-court exercises – which, if you copy them, will prepare you perfectly for top class competition.

I start with strokes that do not demand too much stretching. Muscles may be stiff: you must take care that damage will not be done. Stand at the back and hit the ball up and down the wall (see diagram 17). It is always a good idea to start and finish exercises with lengths, because these are the basis of squash.

Hit the front wall just above the service line, bringing the ball back to bounce just behind the service box. Do several of these, to warm up, and then move back and hit the ball off the back wall. Now move forward a little, still repeating the stroke, and gradually move further and further towards the front wall. Then back again. You must return the ball to yourself, all the time, from different distances.

This one single routine teaches you so much –

Diagram 17. Practice – where the ball is made to bounce just behind the service box. It is taken first before it hits the back wall, and next time after hitting it

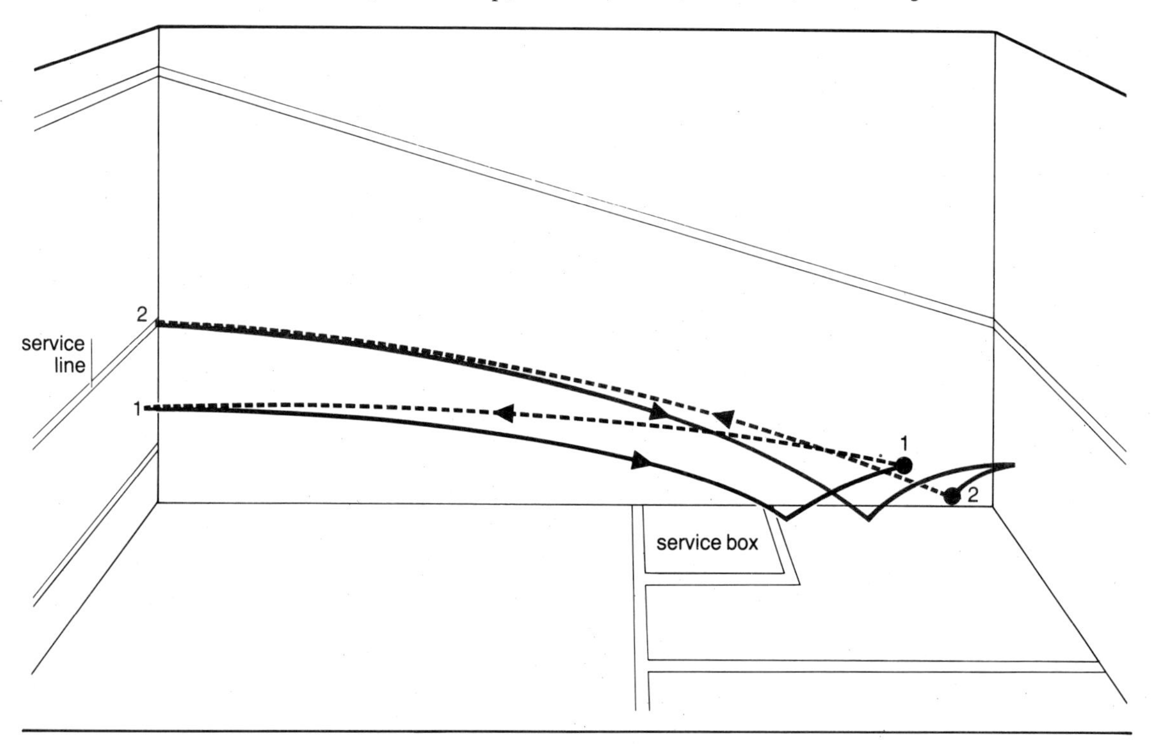

control, how to slice the ball, and how to strike it from different parts of the court. Go right forward and right back again. Then start on the cross-courts. Now you can develop the different impact points. Note the two impact points for a down-the-wall shot – normal (photo 25), from behind the body (photo 14) – and for a cross-court shot (photo 26).

Low and Hard

I stand each side and hit cross court. Five minutes as low and hard as possible is excellent practice. Use maximum power, sending the ball just above the tin, and returning it precisely to your practice partner. The ball does not go to the back of the court, but I hit the ball as though I am trying to get it there. A great deal of strength goes into it although I can also acquire a lot of feeling too. It can also become very hard physically.

Then I hit volleys: high volleys from the same position. This is useful practice for return-of-serve. I hit the ball standing *behind* the service box to two feet below the outline on the front wall. The ball goes to the partner on his backhand and he hits the ball the same way back to the forehand. I try to continue this rally without mistakes: cross-court volleys. Having practised the low shot and then this one, we swap sides.

Next, I move forward to the cut line and do more volleying. The discipline here is to achieve control by trying to hit the service line. After doing this without mistakes I use very short hard volleys, and without stopping, change positions.

After that, I stand on the T with the partner at the back of the court, who throws the ball to the front court on the forehand. I hit a good hard down-the-wall drive right to the back, maintaining control over where the ball bounces. It must land at the back or just behind the service box, and the second bounce should land on or near the back wall nick. This is a perfect length. I try to do that repeatedly.

From the 'T' into the Nick

I return to the T, and as the partner throws a length ball on to the service box move from the T to hit the ball. This is an important shot. About seventy per cent of the time in a match you are moving from the T to this sort of ball. It usually bounces quite high, perhaps about waist height. Both players wil be trying to hit a length from this position, bringing the ball to the back court again and again.

Next, the partner plays the side wall boast and I hit cross court with my backhand on to his forehand. A good hard cross-court shot should bounce just behind the service box. This time, though, I try to put the ball into the nick. Then the ball will roll along the floor and the point is won.

If the ball doesn't roll then we continue, with the partner hitting forehand boasts with me trying to hit a backhand drive nick. Whatever is practised on the backhand should always be done on the forehand. Then change: I go back and hit the boast while the partner hits the ball cross court. He will direct the ball to somewhere behind me, sometimes lobbing to the back, sometimes hitting hard, just as it would be in a match.

In this exercise the partner is not looking for the nick, but trying to make it as difficult as possible. I take the ball off the back wall and hit it on to the side wall. These shots (boasts) can be of different types. There is, for instance, a three-wall boast, which hits the forehand side wall, the front wall and then the backhand side wall. This will go as close to the nick in the backhand front corner as possible, and sometimes, hopefully it will be a nick. It is, though, hit from a defensive situation (photos 40 and 41). Another boast is to hit hard on to the side wall near the short line, thus moving the opponent rapidly to the front court (see photo 35). If performed with a late movement of the wrist, it will start the opponent in the wrong way. It will not be aimed directly at the nick but so that the second bounce goes into the nick. (Note how photographs 36 and 37 show the preparation and impact of the shot on the backhand, and from the front. See photo 39 showing the shot from above and photo 38 from behind.)

The first of these shots may come away from the side wall again but the second boast should get the opponent reaching for the ball as it disappears into the side wall. He will find it is going away from him all the time. He may try to return it just before the second bounce and find the ball is so close to the wall that he will make a mistake, or put up a feeble shot. This second boast is attempted off a shorter ball than the first.

Volleying Exercises

After that, I will go to the back of the court again. The partner will lob and I will volley the ball overhead, once again boasting into the forehand side wall. This is sometimes a good variation on return-of-service. Then I move forward to the T and do the same from there: overhead volley boast. These are attacking shots.

In the next exercise the partner will be standing in the backhand corner at the front. I will be on the T and he will hit cross court just above the service line. That will give me a volley at waist height and I will hit that ball on to the front wall, which is practice for moving the opponent from the front court to the back court with a good length. But instead I will move to return the ball myself, taking it off the back wall and boasting it. Almost at the same time as I boast, I start to go forward, thus practising a movement to the T.

The partner will continue hitting cross court and then he will lob the ball to test an overhead. In the same way I will hit the ball onto the front wall to a good length and then move to boast the ball and recover to the T position.

The partner can do exactly the same thing towards the forehand when I am in the back corner and practising boasts to the front. He hits cross court from the front backhand corner. I will hit down the wall and from my own shot will take the ball off the back wall and boast it. When the ball is cut off, it is usually done either with a volley drive to the back or boast to the front. I stay in the front and the partner will be at the back. He boasts the ball on the forehand to my backhand in the front. I play a drop, he runs to it, and hits a backhand down the wall. I run to the back court and hit a backhand boast on to his forehand in the front, and he drops the ball on the forehand; then I run to the front and hit a forehand down the wall.

All Four Corners

It is an exhausting routine, a four-corner exercise, which embodies the essence of squash. I practise the boast, the drop shot and the down-the-wall length, and move to the four furthest places on the court. It is almost as though I am under pressure in a match. With other exercises I can play long rallies and not really be stretching that much to the four corners. But with this, if I have a long rally of fifty strokes, it is bound to be tough.

There is another tough exercise: I stand on the T and the practice partner throws the ball on to his forehand front corner, almost like a drop shot. I run to the ball from the T and hit as low and as hard as I can and then move back to the T. Just as I reach the T, the partner throws another ball and continues doing that. For the second phase, he plays cross court towards the nick on to my backhand. I run to the ball and take it almost out of the nick, which will produce a very short quick bounce. I hit cross court as hard as I can and as soon as I reach the T, he will throw the ball again.

For the next phase, I will be right at the back wall – by the door – and he tosses the ball just like a soft drop shot on to the front wall. I run to the ball and hit down the wall to a good length, making the ball bounce behind the service box. In these exercises I will be moving backwards and also jumping; actually hopping to the side. It strengthens the legs in a way that won't happen in a match.

If I can do this, then it will be easier for me to run straight to the T. When I reach the back wall the partner throws the ball again. This time it won't really be a drop shot but contacts the wall just under the service line. However, because it is very soft, coming straight down like a lob, it hits the floor and stays there instead of coming back down the court. Therefore it takes me right to the front wall – an awfully long way. When I get there I try to hit a really hard length.

In another exercise I go to the backhand side wall near the cut line and the partner throws the ball on to the forehand side so that it bounces on to the service box. I run towards the ball which is coming down the side wall and try to hit a length. Normally in the game I would be moving from the T, but in this exercise I have to cover twice that distance. Move from side wall to side wall, then run backwards to the backhand side wall. Do this on both sides.

Pressure Training

There is another exercise that I call 'pressure training'. I stand on the T, the practice partner stands near the side and will throw the ball into the forehand front court – like a drop shot. I run to the ball and hit a forehand down the wall but it quickly reaches the partner standing on the cut line. I try to return to the T, but without allowing me time to do so he will boast the ball to my backhand in the front court. I get there as quickly as possible and hit a backhand cross court and then he will again play the ball on to my forehand drop shot. He is moving to the forehand in the front, then to the backhand, with little interval between. This becomes really tough.

After this we do an exercise to cover three different areas of the court. I go to stand behind the service box at the back and he lobs the ball from the front court on to my forehand, down the wall. I hit overhead on to the side wall, a boast, and he lobs the ball on to my backhand. I move from there on to the backhand side and boast the ball on that side too.

We keep doing this for a while, and then I move to the T and he plays a low ball almost on to the service line. It will be a low volley for me but I will still boast on to the side wall. This time, though, it will be much quicker. I will be hitting the ball from both sides, first boasting on the forehand and then moving towards the backhand. The partner hits the volley down the wall to me. Then he drops the ball down the wall right in the front and I move there after one bounce, and play a trickle boast. Then he hits the ball on to the forehand and I move there and boast it on to the backhand. We keep doing this so that we cover three areas, one right at the back, one on the T and one right in the front.

Drop Shot Practices

Next we go through the drop shots. I will usually stand on the T while the partner throws the ball on to the front wall and I hit it so that it bounces into the side wall nick. I will play a backhand, and he suddenly changes the ball on to the other side. Then I play a forehand cross-court drop shot. Next, I get backhand and forehand alternately and finally each side unpredictably so that I don't know which side the ball is coming from.

Next, I leave the T and play drops down the wall towards the cut line – straight drops on the backhand. The he tosses the ball in the air and I will play a volley drop from the same position. I return to the T and he plays a fast boast which goes across the front wall. I really have to stretch for this and try to play a cross-court nick drop shot, recovering immediately to the T. Then I will go for another fast boast and try the same again. This is good for fitness, but it has to be done quickly.

After I have practised several of these on the forehand, I play a straight drop shot. Next, I have to go for another boast, then receive a straight drop and reply in kind, continuing to cover ground like this, always moving to the T between shots.

The next shot I play is the volley, possibly my strongest shot. It may not be yours, but try to play it into the nick. Have the ball fed to you, one backhand, one forehand. Then higher, then overhead, so that you are smashing the ball on the backhand straight on the front wall and into the nick, followed by forehand cross-court nicks. Then do the same on the other side.

Practising Alone

Try to practise these routines every day. A few can be done alone. Face the forehand front corner, standing in front of the short line, and volley a backhand on to the front wall across to the side wall so that it comes on to the forehand. Then volley with the forehand on to the side wall across to the side wall and on to the backhand again. Do this in a corner for some minutes, keeping the ball in the air. It is a good practice session for volleys.

I do the same thing allowing the ball to bounce. The routine and discipline here is that only one leg moves. Keep one leg where it is and move the other to the ball each time. If the ball is on the forehand move the left foot to play and on the backhand side take the left foot back. Play with the 'wrong' foot on one side and the 'correct' foot on the other. It's a stretch, but when an opponent does something unexpected, that is the way it is. Next, change round so that the right leg is moved in the same way. It is an interesting and unusual exercise.

I quite often practise on my own, and so should you. I stand on the T, throw the ball on to the front wall and play a drop shot. I don't recommend too much of this because on the court it is better that you be a 'killer' and not a 'feeder'. If you feed a lot you can get into bad habits. But there will be times when it is unavoidable.

We spoke just now of the exercise where I play off the 'wrong' foot. Many professionals talk about 'correct footwork' but that is usually not how they themselves play. In any squash match, from the top players downwards, you will see many shots played off the wrong foot, especially in the front court.

That is why it is necessary to analyse what really happens and not what was taught many years ago. If you are a beginner, by all means start by learning the 'correct' way, so that you have the best opportunities for balance, control, and progress. But once you have acquired these you can do almost anything you wish. It's a little like driving: learn the correct way, but once you are proficient you act instinctively.

Unorthodox If Need Be

Don't stick rigidly to any text book. A squash player with ability develops initiative in situations where something different is needed. There will be times when a player will be unable to get the correct foot forward or move into the right position. That doesn't mean making a mistake or returning a weak shot. Simply adapt. This can be practised.

For instance, there is one situation where you *must* go for the ball with the wrong foot – one I have mentioned before. That is the forehand deep from the back court. Do a chassis movement and go in with the right ('wrong'!) foot first (see photo 15). That leaves the whole of the front wall open, giving the option for both the cross-court and straight return. It is also possible to play a drop. Notice that on the supposedly correct foot, with the left across, the view of the front wall and of the opponent is hidden. Using the wrong foot also enables you to recover more quickly. But don't do it on the backhand.

Sometimes long strides are needed to be able to retrieve the ball. But not all the time. It would stretch the body unnecessarily. If an opponent creates a surprise with a good drop, three long strides are usually enough to get there. Often though it is better to take steps which are comfortable. These will depend on the individual. Much of the time I recover to the T with small steps. However it is better to think less about whether to use a short or long stretch and concentrate on anticipating the actions of the opponent. It is essential to move quickly.

One exercise I do quite often is boasting by myself. Standing on the T, I hit the ball on to the side wall on the short line, over towards the backhand. I go and retrieve it after one bounce, then boast it over to the forehand side again. I try to retrieve the ball repeatedly.

One Volley, One Boast, One Lob

In another routine, my practice partner lobs from the front court on to my backhand. I hit down the wall on the volley and move to the T, he boasts and then I lob, so that he has to volley the ball down the wall. We are therefore practising one high volley down the wall, one boast and one lob from the front. Each player does this alternately. Practise this a lot.

Sometimes I play against two players, just an open game but a proper game. This can be very tough, especially if the two opponents have an understanding. Then it becomes almost as demanding as doing 440s with small recovery intervals. It often produces rapid improvements.

What I have tried to illustrate here and in the chapter on 'hitting' is that there are three dimensions to the court – length, width and height. Exercises and practices are needed for all of them. These should begin at the front of the court and move back. There are shots at knee, waist and head height, and shots down the wall, cross-court boasts, drops and lengths. Practise them all on forehand and backhand. All kinds of shot-making in all situations should then be grooved.

KHAN'S

CONQUESTS V

JAHANGIR KHAN BEATS RODNEY MARTIN
9-6, 10-8, 9-1;
BRITISH OPEN FINAL, WEMBLEY 1990

This was the win that gave me the record ninth British Open title. It was also the success that many said might not happen. My build-up had been the least impressive it had ever been. I was heavier than usual, and in the last tournament before my attempt on the record, the Spanish Open, I had been beaten in straight games by Rodney Martin.

I had been concerned about that loss. But I believed I knew how to peak for the big occasion. After all, this was something Hunt himself had often done. He had even been known to lose all his build-up tournaments and still win the British Open. I knew I was capable of the same, despite many of the predictions. And between Madrid and Wembley there had been four weeks in which to get into shape.

I had used those to work extra hard in training, which, of course, few people could know. My weight had come down, my confidence had gone up, and my stamina had improved. I was sure I could be a different player by the time the British Open final was played, and that if I did my best I would be good enough to have a chance again.

Certainly my father thought so, for he made the journey from Karachi to London for the first time in 25 years. Many thought they would never see him at a British Open again, and it was a surprise to me too that he decided to come to watch. When he had won in 1957 he earned £50 and 30 people watched. Now there was a £8000 first prize and 3000 spectators. Although his presence raised expectations it was also a help to have his support at the courtside.

My belief that I could win if I timed my preparation properly, and that I might have got this right, had been strengthened by my results in the previous rounds. I had not dropped a game and conceded only 40 points in four matches. Playing Martin in a final might be a far tougher proposition than any of these. But as before I resolved to set up a high-paced attack, and to keep the ball tight to deny him room for his most damaging strokes.

The first game went well. I won the first point with a penalty stroke, and after both of us had acknowledged balls that were down, I got to 4-2. A good spell got me to 6-3 and he still seemed a little nervous. Twice he tinned the ball, enabling me to reach game ball at 8-3. Then at last he dug in and got back to 6-8 after I had been refused two lets. Still, he hit another tin to give me the first game in 31 minutes.

Even in the early stages of the second game he was having difficulty in producing his best, and a run of errors gave me a five-point cushion. This was extremely valuable because soon Martin was back to 4-5, and revealing his determination by getting cross at the referee for the refusal of two lets. He was fitter than he used to be and may have reckoned he was fitter than me, because he appeared to be trying to rally with me and to make me run. But I got to 6-4 and 7-5, and reached game ball at 8-5 with a hard forehand volley that found the nick and rolled satisfyingly.

Then came the match's one brief crisis. I missed a drop and Martin hit a winning volley and suddenly it was 7-8. He was working very hard and got to 8-8. Then I had two more game balls at 9-8 only for him to save those as well.

All of a sudden he made an error and threw his racket up in the air. Then I knew he was still very tense. He was refused a let and once more the racket was hurled upwards, this time to fall with a clatter to the floor. Martin's concentration was not good and another mistake gave me the game 10-8. The match was virtually over.

In the third game I got to 8-0 in one run. His only point came from a penalty stroke and after little more than an hour and a quarter's effort I had won. I bowed down to God. My father was first into the court to embrace me. My dream had come true.

When Martin had most needed his best it was

not there. By contrast when my biggest test had come, so too had my best squash.

Lesson Peak for your most important matches.

CHAPTER 6

EXCELLING

Anyone who has followed the suggestions made in this book should now be a good player. Don't stop at that. Great things are achieved by those who keep going. It's worth trying to go all the way. It's worth becoming a champion. The world is full of people who regret not knowing how good they might have been.

It takes many, varied and subtle things to become an advanced player. It requires developing a style, a way of playing that suits your character, abilities, and strengths. That will quickly become apparent. First, though, there are more shots to think about, shots that add variety to a repertoire.

Diagram 18. Reverse angle. This is hit hard and fast across the body from a ball short of a length with the opponent behind. It looks as though it may be a forehand drive/kill until the last moment change of direction

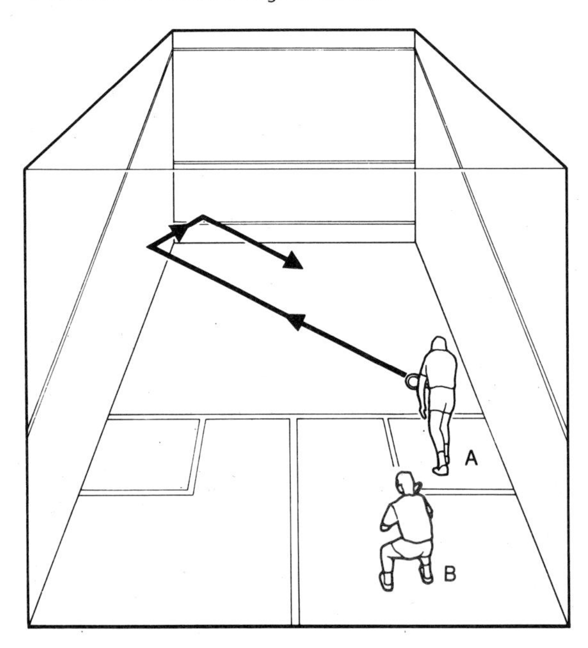

Combinations of advanced shots have been discussed in the court exercises. It is by using these combinations cleverly that one finishes off opponents. The forehand cross-court into the nick after your opponent has boasted, for instance, mixed with a punishing forehand straight kill, is particularly effective. Combine the two with a little trickle boast, playing it round from the side wall to the front wall in the forehand front corner, and the opponent will never be sure what is going to happen next. He may move into a different position each time. If you become aware of this while you play your shot – listen carefully and use your lateral vision – then he can be made to guess wrongly each time.

The Reverse Angle

Another variation is the reverse angle. This brings the ball short but has the advantage of being struck as hard as a drive, thus lessening the likelihood of depositing it into the tin. (Some players are afraid of this on the drop shot). The reverse angle is best used when the opponent fails to make a full length. After shaping up to play another drive to a length, a change of direction of the shot is made at the last moment.

Instead of hitting the ball down the wall, the wrist is turned to strike it firmly across the body. The ball goes across the court to hit the side wall low, about a foot from the front wall, and it then shoots hard back across court quite short (see diagram 18). If executed properly it will wrong-foot the opponent and tire him to retrieve it. Sometimes it is an outright winner. The second bounce can go unpleasantly close to the other side wall as the opponent is trying to reach for it.

The reverse angle is usually executed most easily with the forehand because the arm and the wrist more comfortably come across the body, bringing about the unexpected change of direction. On the backhand the arm does not bend easily in a cross-court direction, so more of the deception comes from the wrist. But it can still be done effectively, especially if it looks as though you are going to drive the ball across court, and only a slight change of direction sends the ball flying back the other way. I used this shot more as my career progressed.

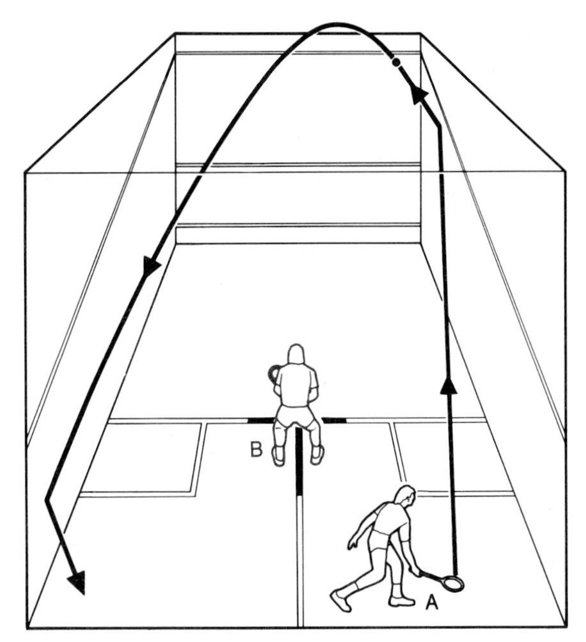

Diagram 19. The skid boast is useful both as a surprise and as a shot to get out of trouble from a position where it may be difficult to boast. It must pass high over the opponent on the T otherwise it can be cut off for a winner. It is more likely to become a winner itself if the opponent is edging forward expecting a drop shot for a boast. If it succeeds it will drop right into the backhand back corner

The Skid Boast

Some players also find the skid boast useful. This skids high off the side wall near the front and diagonally over the centre of the court high into the opposite back corner (see diagram 19). It is a strange shot and needs to be played perfectly if the opponent is not to be given an easy mid-court volley. But Gogi Alauddin always used it very well, and so have an increasing number of players.

A good time to try it is when your opponent has played a very deep shot to the back corner in the forehand. It is best used on that side because it needs power to play the skid boast safely, and the forehand is normally the more powerful side. You will want to use it when the ball is so deep that you have difficulty hitting straight to the front wall, and when you don't want to hit a conventional boast because your opponent is well forward on the T, waiting. Use your wrist and strike under the ball as hard and as high as you can. Ideally it will go on to the side wall about three feet from the front wall, skid on to the front wall one foot below the out line and sail rapidly over your opponent's head into the back corner. It is a defensive shot but it can turn into a winner, particularly if the opponent moves too early into the front court believing you can only hit a hard low boast.

It is an unusual shot and there have been players prepared to invent other unusual shots. I would never discourage a good player from doing that. Most players have one or two shots at which they are particularly clever, and sometimes they produce them in an unusual way. There was a time when nobody used to play a topspin drop shot. But this can be deceptive, especially when it gives the impression that it is a drive or a cross-court. Even now coaches sometimes advise not to play a drop shot from the back of the court. That is nonsense.

Done well that can have an enormous element of surprise. Do whatever you like, so long as you can regularly create an advantage with it.

The Half-volley

Another unorthodox shot worth having is the half-volley. If the timing is right and it is played accurately, it is often a very surprising return because the opponent cannot read it. An excellent topspin drop shot can be produced as a half-volley. There is a whole variety of drop shots that can be played with the half-volley, especially when your opponent is at the back, stretching, and decides to hit across court. If the ball bounces short, playing a quick half-volley boast, which Torsam used to do quite a lot, will have your opponent in trouble. He will not have enough time to get it because he won't expect the ball to be cut off in that way.

The Tight Retrieve

An unorthodoxy which is increasingly used at top level is shortening the grip, in order to get the ball out of a tricky situation deep in the backhand corner. You need to be facing the back wall, and to flick the ball over or past your right shoulder (see photos 64 and 65).

Perhaps you can do all these things we have described; perhaps you can't. Develop your own strengths. But it is very instructive to learn from the strengths of other great players. You may be able to copy from them and develop something similar but, more important, you will get a sense of how they consolidated their strengths around their particular types of ability, physique, and character. Among the many that have been worth studying have been Rodney Martin for his ability to cut the ball into the nick, Jansher Khan for his ability to

64. Backhand retrieve preparation The grip has been moved up the handle. The back is turned to the front wall. This is done because there is little room and time

65. Backhand retrieve – impact The wrist is bent to compensate for lack of space. Notice how close the racket head is to the back wall

contain opponents' attack, Chris Dittmar for his balance between the short and the long games, and Geoff Hunt for his mental strength. As I say, these qualities cannot be exactly reproduced. But insight into how they evolved will certainly help you develop your own abilities.

Jansher Khan

Sometimes called JK Mark II. Although his playing style and personality are completely different from mine, there are one or two interesting similarities in his development. Like myself, he had an elder brother who was a leading professional, and like me he suffered family tragedy. Like me, too, he successfully set out to realise his brother's frustrated ambition to be world champion (Mohibullah Khan was world number two).

Similarly, he shut himself away in a flat in London (Mohammed Yasin's), except for when he was training or practising. In six months' disciplined hard work he had turned himself from a good and promising player into one of the best in the world. Jansher was only a little older than I when, at the age of 18, he became world champion.

There is much to be learnt from this, about the single-mindedness necessary to make the top, how best to achieve that, and the increasingly early age at which it is necessary.

Jansher is probably at his best as a containing player. This does not necessarily mean that he is defensive. But he is often most effective when he is involved in long rallies to a length, with his opponent trying to force the pace.

This is because he has a well produced basic drive which is so excellently grooved that he can repeat it for long periods under pressure without mistakes. It is also because he has such a slim, light build, and such economical footwork, that he can move to the corners and recover to the T with exceptional speed. This can be done in a variety of ways, but he usually does so with a short, quick-stepping method that can create the impression that he is doing little more than walking.

This is not so of course. Jansher's well-practised court coverage is skilful, balanced, and an important ingredient in his success. He has been adding other ingredients and there has been a marked improvement in Jansher's ability to attack. In certain moods against certain opponents he can take them on and punish them severely for anything loose, with fiercely struck drives and neat wall-clinging drops.

He has developed his volleys too, and sometimes plays whole tournaments where this aspect of his game also looks highly competent. Under physical pressure, however, and sometimes when it matters most, his volleying can occasionally still be suspect.

Surprisingly, so can his ability to soak up mental pressure. When he first came on the scene Jansher would play long matches, come from behind, and outlast opponent after opponent. Recently though he has sometimes shown signs of losing heart and failing to battle out the hard matches. It is this that has caused questions about whether he will remain at the top of the game for as long as his ability suggests he should.

Rodney Martin

Rodney Martin, like myself, comes from a well-known squash family – his brother Brett and sister Michelle have both been top ten players – but in other ways we are completely different. I have tried to base my game in an orthodox way on good length and good physical condition and being patient if necessary before going for the openings. Martin can be a law unto himself in the way he seeks and makes openings, sometimes from nowhere.

Not that his basic technique is unorthodox. Indeed he could not get away with some of the extraordinary strokes he attempts, but for superb preparation and a beautifully grooved racket path, as well as an outstanding eye for the ball. Some of his feel for the ball comes from his grip. Look at it – fingers sensitively positioned, pressure gently but firmly applied to the handle, and maximum sympathy with the racket generated.

Martin has the reputation of being the finest strokemaker in the game since Qamar Zaman in the mid-eighties. He ought to concentrate on this, not only because this is the way to please crowds and an exciting way to win titles. It is also because there have sometimes been less pleasant elements that have crept into his matches with me, such as unnecessary pushing and shoving to help his accusations of blocking. This indicates something of the increased pressures and incentives to succeed at the top.

What has been impressive, though, is the development in Martin's game. In his earlier days he depended a lot – perhaps too much – on finding openings for his razor-sharp volley, especially the backhand volley. With this he steps forward and find the nick with cutting regularity. He does this with a smoother action than Zaman, who used to jerk at the ball, creating more disguise, but providing a riskier model for youngsters to copy.

Martin is now far better at waiting for the openings, because he has worked more on his fitness and can now last a long match better. This gives him more options but also creates more tactical complications. For instance in the 1990 British Open he seemed to have decided he was fitter than I was and that he should try to run me. This was probably a mistake, particularly as he did this to the exclusion of his strokes.

Getting a tactical balance right is important and not always easy, especially as Martin has, by his own admission, been unusually nervous on the big occasions. Judgement and temperament may or may not remain a problem for him, but on his day there is no doubt he can be the most dangerous player of all.

Chris Dittmar

Dittmar has had the reputation of being a creative player who also knows how to make life enjoyable. It has been the way he has changed his outlook, learnt to work hard, and develop his abilities further than seemed possible, which has been the most admirable thing about him.

When Dittmar reached his first World Open final, against me back in 1983, he possessed a ferocious forehand, a far less aggressive backhand, and the need to go for all sorts of exotic shots at the front because he did not have the capacity to play out a long match. Admittedly he had the skill to attempt this, and it sometimes won him spectacular games, as in the one game he took from me in the 1986 World Open. But it did not make him a great threat and in those days he rarely looked like winning a big title when I was playing.

Then came a serious knee injury that put him out of the game for more than a year. It gave him time to reassess himself and to decide his priorities in life. Having a good time became less important, and improving and maintaining his fitness far more so. His injury left him unable to train in the normal way, and perhaps this gave him a better appreciation of how precious good physical condition is to a player.

Certainly Dittmar learnt to last the course far better than ever he did before. He acquired the dedication to work whilst imprisoned within four walls, using bicycles and rowing machines to protect his knee against repeated pounding on the ground. He has developed his body and proved his character, and been rewarded with victories over every leading player in the world.

In the process he has acquired a better weighted game. Instead of fireworks on one side and software on the other, he has a more solid drive on both wings, with greater accuracy on the backhand, and better ability to deliver sharp changes of pace on the forehand. He has developed disguise and a wider range of options with both. And he has cleverly covered up weaknesses in certain areas in the front of the court, caused by the damage to his knee.

Most notable of all, he has developed an excellent balance between the short and the long games. Dittmar's ball control is so precise that he can choose far better than most when to play short, and when to shape short but play long. And his judgement of when to use each has become better and better as the years go by.

Dittmar is the same age as me, and has several times narrowly missed the two major titles, the World and British Open. One wonders if he will remain one of the best never to have won either.

Money

Most players need to provide for themselves financially while they are training, and so a very large number of non-British players are forced to leave their home country and spend several months of the year in England. They are trying to kill two birds with one stone – looking for competition and at the same time a way to make money. If a player wants the best chance of establishing himself I think he (or she) has to do this. Most of the time, players cannot afford to keep coming to England for tournaments and then going home again. Even before they look to make a living they will be trying to recover what they have spent and pressure will be on them all the time. You can't operate like that. Contracts with companies and sponsors are not easy to come by. Staying in England for several months each year cuts costs considerably.

Many players coach to make money while playing the tournaments, but I don't recommend it. It fosters bad habits. Such players become flat on their feet as well as mentally tired. They may adopt contradictory frames of mind. The coach's attitude is one of giving, and he must give a great deal of himself in the course of a day's work. But the top tournament player must think primarily of himself. He must, as far as playing squash is concerned, be selfish. He must learn to take, if he is to win, not to give.

Many players have to tolerate poverty, living in fourth- and fifth-class hotels, and a great deal of tiring travelling. They should not, it goes without saying, economize on food. Some find it difficult to resist the temptations at the bar. A little adulation and spectators wanting to buy drinks can be delightful – and destructive. Late nights and loneliness are a major problem too. It is difficult for a young person to stay disciplined. That's also why many players need coaches, managers, and partners if they can find them.

Avoiding Injuries

Injuries can also be a major pitfall. At the top level the body will be pushed harder than ever before. No-one can know how it will react. Sometimes players feel they cannot afford treatment and try to play through injuries, afraid to miss the chance of earning money. Usually this is a false economy. Other players overtrain. Try to assess your limits and build up your training over a period of months rather than go for short-term gains.

Tiredness, jet lag, and planning and peaking for the major events present further problems. So do people who come up and talk and ask questions before matches. Keep away from them and try to empty your mind of distractions before you play. Take a few days' break before a tournament in which you need to do particularly well.

What you may notice both before and after matches involving leading players is competitors performing an assortment of exercises in the changing room, the corridors and other places. Warming up and warming down are of the utmost importance for performance and fitness. Most players warm up but not everybody warms down. Muscles that suddenly cool become stiff and are susceptible to injury, and they need to be sufficiently stretched without being over-extended. So don't sit down after a match when you are hot and sweaty: do some stretching.

If possible, take a complete break from squash

for two months every year. Go swimming, or take some other form of exercise. Light weight-training is excellent to develop body strength. During the long tournament season this is sometimes neglected, and it may be necessary to make up for it.

A break between seasons can be an important time for stocktaking. After my defeat in the 1981 British Open final, I took a break from the game and rethought my whole training programme. With Rahmat Khan I then built up for the World Open final six months later, which I won.

The Need for a Coach

There are plenty of players with natural talent and good ball control who still don't succeed. Often this is because such players need clear objectives and simple directives before they go on court. By all means think deeply and about complicated matters when you are away from the action, but a clear plan should come from your theorizing. Keep it nice and simple in your head just before you go on court.

One important advantage of a coach is that he can see two players on the court. The competitor can only see one. This obvious point is sometimes forgotten. A coach can also decide to watch one of the players all the time, whether that player is hitting the ball or not. Much can be learned from this. It is possible to see what happens when he is not striking the ball, how far he recovers to the T, what positions he takes up, what expressions and feelings he displays, and whether or not he is tired. All this can be most revealing. At these 'non-playing' moments the player believes he is on his own. He knows the gallery watches when he hits the ball, but may feel he is not observed in the moments between shots. Then he may reveal himself.

It can be valuable to discuss with a coach what to expect from an opponent. However, what happens on court can be quite different from even the most perceptive analysis. If so, the end of the first game is the most important time in the whole match: well enough into the action to get an idea of what is really happening but not too late to do something about it. That's when a coach, if he can think and talk quickly and knows his stuff, can be effective.

Psychology

Occasionally good players do well and then go to pieces. This is sometimes caused by thinking about what *might* happen. Such an attitude is not dissimilar to that of the player who is sure he will lose even before he is on the court. Do not be afraid to win and do not be afraid to lose. Better still, do not consider either of them. Keep your mind on the training you have done. Concentrate on what you are going to do next. Take one point at a time. Don't give up.

There are usually crucial moments in a close match when one of the players begins to feel the pressure and becomes vulnerable. Then the match can turn. It is vital to keep thinking that your opponent is feeling just as bad. Never imagine you are alone in your tiredness.

Learn to observe the movements of your opponent and see what he likes and doesn't like. Watch his technique and what he attempts. If he is keeping the ball low and fast he may still have plenty of energy, but if he is sending the ball high then he may not want a fast game. If he is attempting plenty of strokes rather than long rallies this too may be an indication of tiredness.

If an opponent is getting slower, try to make him run. Try to hit a little harder to the back of the court, volley more if you can, and then take him to the front by boasting. Don't give him time to recover. This is how breakthroughs are achieved. Pressure applied at the right time can save you great trouble from an opponent who might recover. But don't choose the drop unless it is the obvious shot. Better to tire him first.

Hidden Ability

I have talked just a little about preparing for a match, but in reality this is a big, difficult, complicated matter. Whether he knows it or not, everybody has a power within him, a power that can bring out hidden ability. It helps to become aware that you can achieve a great deal more than you ever realized. This is not magic, although occasionally it does seem like it.

Some people try to bring the latent ability out by hypnotism or hypnotherapy. This in fact is what I did. It relaxes the body, concentrates the mind, and clears it of unnecessary worries. By concentrating better you acquire the ability to think positively. After a while you can detach yourself and achieve a mental state in which the unconscious starts to take over. This has been described as like being on automatic pilot. It is in this state that you can often do things without wholly realizing it, and do them very well. Only afterwards do you become completely aware of what has happened.

Being in this frame of mind is a little like praying. The body relaxes: the worries have gone. It is pressure that prevents your mind from thinking positively about what you want to achieve. Pressure stunts ability. Pressure is the problem in many areas of life. It divides the mind. And the body reacts to the mind.

Prayer, hypnotism, meditation, yoga and other different forms of relaxation are all part of the same thing, though not many people realize it. Nor do they realize how these meditative exercises can be practised in just a moment or two, between doing one thing and starting the next, even when the hurly-burly of life is at its greatest. An enhanced mental state, such as these methods achieve, is of enormous value to a squash player who may need to use his mind to drag his body to the limits.

I can promise you that nothing does this quite so effectively as prayer, which takes time and effort and discipline and practice. Prayer is a complete refresher.

KHAN'S CONQUESTS VI

JAHANGIR KHAN BEATS JANSHER KHAN
2-9, 9-4, 9-4, 9-0;
BRITISH OPEN FINAL, WEMBLEY 1991

Although I had already achieved the record of nine titles there were a few people still prepared to question the achievement because I had not played a British Open final against Jansher Khan since he first became world champion late in 1987.

Jansher topped the rankings more often than anyone else in the next three years and also won the most tournaments around the world. But for some reason he had yet to produce his best in a British Open, and there were some who thought that when this happened he could beat me.

However, although he reached the final for the first time for four years, I beat him in a match well contested enough to last an hour and 35 minutes. I did so, I believe, not only because I was again able to peak physically for the most important tournament, as I had the year before against Rodney Martin, but because my mental preparation and condition were better than Jansher's. This too can make the difference between winning and losing.

It had not been easy to achieve this. On doctor's advice I had spent more than four months away from the circuit, at the start of which I had wondered whether I would actually be able to compete seriously again. I had experienced major changes in my life – including a long, large and highly publicized wedding, which was as big a test of pressure as any British Open! Also the enforced break inevitably saw the return of the problem of weight gain.

By complete contrast Jansher went seven months without losing a tournament, the best run of his career. He was the top seed for the second time at Wembley.

Despite this I knew I was the unofficial favourite and would have a good chance if I could produce my best when it mattered. And I had extra reasons for thinking I could. I had a new and lucrative contract with Estusa which increased my financial security. I had my father Roshan Khan and national coach Umar Draz Khan with me to give support and advice. I had organized my training to continue through the build-up tournaments, and yet I had still managed to win two of them.

All this meant that I had a well-structured life and a confident frame of mind, even though I had had a lot of ground to make up on my closest rivals, and some people had been writing me off completely.

I had doubts about Jansher's mental strength. True, he had won the World Open a third time, a fine achievement, but he had shown signs of falling away when the pressure had been kept upon him. He had a complicated private life which was attracting public attention, had changed managers, which had also caused some friction, and was finding it difficult to land all the commercial contracts which he felt his squash deserved. He was a great player but not the greatest organized. This might make a difference.

Sure enough, when I kept the pressure on him, he could not maintain a response. Early on, he looked as though he could win the British Open for the first time. He won the first game in 23 minutes, although many of the rallies had not been of the highest pace and Jansher seemed content to play the ball up and down the wall. He had not grabbed many opportunities to take the initiative.

In the second game I decided to take them. I was a game and 0-2 down when I found the room and the angle to hit a forehand volley into the nick. It rolled satisfyingly across the floor. I followed it with a near perfect drop shot winner, and after that I was on my way.

I was able to make Jansher hurry more. Although he usually likes opponents to come at him, I sensed that he might not respond to it so well on this occasion. After getting my nose in front in the second game I continued to attack and this was followed by errors from Jansher that were both forced and unforced.

Jansher started the third by putting the ball into the tin – a great sign for me. I produced another couple of good drops and was rewarded with a 3-0 lead and a mistake from Jansher on the next rally that suggested how much pressure must be affecting his state of mind. He drove the ball straight into the floor, a rare piece of mistiming that helped convince me I could win and that my approach was right. A continued policy of sensible aggression earned me chances for two more nicks that I attacked vigorously, making the ball hurtle along the floor again. On game ball Jansher once more hit the tin.

I started the fourth game with another nick, this time from deep on the forehand side. That seemed to confirm my control. After it the match became a procession. Jansher lobbed out, and I found more winners with a forehand nick, a perfect killing forehand and a high backhand volley into the nick.

Jansher had cracked. In only a few more moments two more winners from me and two more mistakes from him had brought the end of the match. My father was on the court, hugging me. Umar Draz was applauding. I felt I had proved a point.

I had also established a place in history. I was for all time the record-holder of the twentieth century. If anyone were to beat my ten British Opens, it would not be until the next century that they would do it!

Lesson: Mental fitness, as well as physical.

CHAPTER 7

HOW YOU TOO CAN BECOME WORLD CHAMPION

People sometimes ask why I don't talk much. It is often because I have too much on my mind. I have worked, I am preparing, I have a goal to achieve. That is how it has to be. Top squash is one of the hardest professions. A leading player has to go through more difficulties, to sacrifice more, and to resist more temptations than almost any other profession in the world.

If a player starts worrying about impressing people socially, he is going to be diverted from the seriousness of his profession. A joker makes everyone laugh – for a time, but when the real star comes on, all the applause is for him. A joker is just a joker. Which do you want to be? You need to make up your mind.

People used to criticize me for not smiling much. You know, a serious actor may create a certain image by his work, but off stage he may be quite different - perhaps a jolly person. I believe I am like that. Sometimes you wouldn't think I was the same man as the Jahangir you see on court. But away from squash I am free in my mind and without important work to do. Responsibility nearly always makes people different. And to become a champion certainly involves responsibility.

Be Single-Minded

To become a champion also requires special character. But don't let that make you give up. There is nothing impossible if one tries hard enough; however you must try very, very hard. Squash requires you to be single-minded – in training, on the court, and off the court alike. If you want to be the boss in anything, you just cannot mix willy-nilly with everyone. This may make you quiet or it may not, but either way it does not make you a bad person.

To succeed you must in every detail do what is right and good for your particular purpose. Don't follow the rest of the world. The rest of the world does not have the ambitions of becoming a champion. Out on the street there are thousands of people; God knows where they are going or what they are doing. You do not have to know. You should be considering only your own destination.

If you don't keep on the right track you will drift and arrive somewhere you didn't wish to be. Whatever one's goal in life, it needs to have been one's own decision. Advice should be sought, of course, and I have already suggested the need for coaching in top-level squash. But then a personal decision must be made about what plan is to be followed, what discipline is needed. Be honest with yourself and with your partner, coach or helper. Then be completely single-minded about the goal.

Loneliness

Loneliness may be one of your biggest enemies. I say that not just because I lost a brother, for whom I often sat down and cried. Loneliness is a problem for many players. After a long hard match or a long session of training it is easy to feel depressed. You go to your hotel room and as soon as you hit the bed you are lonely. It is easy to be tempted by sex, especially when you feel physically healthy. If the opportunity is there you may very well take it.

I am certain this happens to many players. I've seen them unable to sleep because they are in a big hotel and there's a discothèque. The player who gets up and heads for the music knows he is being foolish but he has not enough control or will power to resist. Tomorrow he has a match and he will be tired.

You might as well know what has to be sacrificed if you are to be a champion. No world champion in squash has indulged in drink or sex to any great extent. I was fortunate because I came from Pakistan and a Muslim culture, and no great appetite had been created in me for such things. Media people have asked me about this, hoping for a story, but we really *don't* drink much or go to discothèques. Often the journalists found it hard to believe. I like music, at my home; I like friends. But I am dedicated to my profession. Perhaps others are different. If so, they must strive to create the discipline to succeed.

Avoid Distractions

As I have mentioned before, there are always people who will pester players. When trying to build up your concentration and composure before a match it is essential to avoid them. Try to sit together with a friend or coach before a match and discuss the opponent, refreshing the memory about weaknesses and strengths. This is a great help.

Hide yourself away. If you are in a public place people will approach and say: 'Come on! You've got to win this'. Immediately that creates more responsibility. Someone else says: 'You can do it'. More responsibility. And another: 'It'll be easy'. Such backslappers must be kept away. It can happen that in the middle of a match a picture comes into your mind of the one who said, 'You have to win', followed by the awful thought – what will happen if you don't? The mind can play tricks on you.

Immediately before a match it is best to have a few words about basics, as simply as possible. Avoid technical detail at this stage. I have one excellent method of building up concentration in those tense and difficult moments – ten minutes sitting on the toilet! It's relaxing anyway, but it's a splendid place for thinking about what you are going to do. Quite a few players endorse this wonderful strategy. I recommend it.

Training

A coach can help most of all with training. Given basic ability and basic technique, it is training more than anything that will make a player into a champion. Here is where single-mindedness will reveal itself. Nobody wins without training hard these days. That was what made Geoff Hunt such a great champion, and that was what enabled me to catch him up. This is our last, most-to-be-remembered lesson.

It is essential to realize it is very difficult to do the training necessary to reach the top while still playing tournaments. Time is needed to get into the routine, and also to build up new muscles and strengthen old ones.

Despite this you can prepare yourself for training by analysing your matches. Why were certain matches lost? Why did you get tired? When did you get tired? Which movements did you find most difficult to sustain? Such things should be written down. When the season is over, or when you make a break for yourself, these ideas can be worked on. You must make a plan.

The next thing is to build the necessary basic physical strength. The endurance and stamina needed for the really hard tournaments can only be developed off the court. That is because only off-court training can be arranged so that it does not become boring. Players do train on the court as well, but usually it cannot be sustained for very long. Two or three hours on the court is tough and because it is a small place it is easy to feel confined. After a while the necessary mental effort no longer seems worth it.

I have always tried to go for my training to nice, attractive places, places where it is pleasant for the eyes, where there is fresh air, and a sense of well-being. This is one of the secrets of training. Twice the amount of work can be achieved in these conditions. You can also double the size of your training 'squash court' by marking out the area on the ground and then repeating movements used in matches. When you come back to the real one it will seem like a baby court. It will hardly seem possible that the ball can take two bounces.

Train if you like on a tennis court, but anywhere where there is flat, open ground will do. Then stretch yourself, really stretch yourself, doing shadow exercises without a ball. One way to do these is to number each section of the ground, have someone shout in turn each number you are to move to, and then go back to the T between each movement. This is realistic, yet afterwards the real thing will seem tame by comparison.

The Plan

But – to the plan! I used to get up at 6.00 a.m., sometimes 7.00, always early. Even though it was dark, and the English climate often seemed to me very cold, I would still make an early start. This again is one of my secrets: it is not possible to do all that is required by beginning training late in the day. It is best done before practice or playing: more benefit is obtained that way. Also, time is needed to do all of these things in a day without going to bed late. Late nights mean the recovery will not be the same.

When you are training very hard you often need more sleep than a normal person. Early to bed, early to rise is therefore a vital part of the routine. People without a faith or discipline will find it harder. But quite a few manage it and if you wish to become a champion, so must you. In our faith, you freshen yourself and wash yourself and then bend down and stretch when you pray. Muslim or not, I recommend all of this. It will be good for you as a person and for your training.

Thus washed, refreshed and stretched, you are ready for your run. Now you feel as though you are going to work before everybody else. This can be a good feeling, dark and cold though it may be. A new day is about to be given, and you are not going to waste any of it. Your faith in yourself is strengthened.

I know players go out in the morning without washing. Some even sleep in a track suit so that they just have to put on their runners and go! This is not a good idea. The attitude to work that our method of preparation encourages is far more positive. And the right attitude, in the face of all that hard work and all that discipline, is something you will need if you are not to give up.

Background Work

To begin with do as much jogging as possible, to strengthen the legs. This is background work, but you cannot proceed without it. Without strong legs you cannot work hard. Before going on to sprints you need to have built up ligaments and muscles. Build up patience and endurance at the same time. Then towards the end of the training go on to faster work. That helps give speed around the court, but it will take more out of you, and you cannot continue with it all the time. You will also recover more slowly from it. Therefore it is best to finish with the speed work.

Gradually I built up my running from three to ten miles a day. Whatever you can do and still recover well enough to manage the next day, that is what you should be satisfied with. Then slowly, slowly on to the 440-yard sprints which are extremely hard for a player of any ability.

It was for doing 440s that Geoff Hunt became renowned. They may not suit every type of physique, but if you *are* able to do them they are very valuable for a top squash player. They are well suited to squash at the highest level because they repeat its rhythms.

For instance, if you are involved in a long rally and, as sometimes happens, become trapped and wrong-footed, an opponent with good ball control will start stretching you up and down the court. He may not kill the ball and he may not even want to do so. He may want only to hit it hard enough to start wearing you down. He hits it at medium speed, you stretch, he keeps you going up and down, up and down, and very soon the pain starts to come.

These retrieves, up and down the court, are roughly equivalent to running a 440. To do them you need to be fast, though not necessarily like a bullet. Get the 440 tuned for the speed that fits your standard of squash and see that each sprint is done at that speed. Then get the recovery interval between sprints down from a minute to forty-five seconds, to half a minute, then less. This discipline will serve a player well when the mind is tired and the body is hurting and the temptation is to give up. Hunt at his best would build up to twenty-five or thirty of these 440s with only a small recovery interval.

After doing these in training it is possible, almost no matter what the pain, to keep the ball going. With ordinary players the steps shorten, the concentration goes, the percentage game goes. Ultimately, though, the body can be trained to cope with a tremendous amount of extra strain.

Timetable

Don't do the 440s too early in the morning unless time is pressing and circumstances dictate. The ideal is either jogging early or 440s in the middle of the day, but don't do 440s *and* jogging on the same day. I tend to do a long jog one day, 440s the next and continue this on alternate days. Each day there is a rest and later on I play squash. After my early morning jog, I come back and have my breakfast, but it is also important just to eat a little something before going out. Honey is excellent and perhaps a light cereal to support the body before training.

After a substantial post-jogging breakfast I go on to the court about 11.00 a.m. I will then do the routines with the ball described in chapter 5. Generally I don't worry too much about what I eat. It is important to enjoy your food and I don't believe you should change your diet, unless there is obviously something wrong. I eat exactly what I am used to before big matches. That is the best thing provided you don't eat *immediately* before playing or training.

Combining playing and training cannot be done with any great degree of success. Tournaments and matches tell you only how good you already are. Don't rely on them for improvement. For that, rely on your training. Inevitably sometimes you will find you are not as good as you hoped. As I have described, this happened to me in the British Open final in 1981 when Geoff Hunt came back from apparent exhaustion to win a match of more than two hours.

I was very tired at the end of that match and as I have explained, I went away on a much-needed holiday. At the time nobody blamed me for losing. But when I came back to start training again, criticisms were made. That was how I set to work to build a new fitness and a new engine, one with enough fuel to beat Hunt in the World Open of November that year.

This preparation took six months but I would probably not need to do that now because the foundation work is all there. I would require, perhaps, just two months to prepare for a major tournament. But somebody who has never done it and who is trying to get to the top may well need the six months.

Such a player would have to continue his training on a long-term basis until he had reached his target, always bearing in mind that he must have adequate rest. Without it, believe me, the work will be too much. Make sure you have it and begin fresh each time.

A week in my training would consist of work for five days with different types of running, squash with different players, and practice alone or with a partner. Then I would try to finish with swimming. Swimming can be quite important: it is an exercise in itself, as well as a relaxation. It also helps to prevent injuries and it is so good for the back. A squash player needs a strong back and to develop muscles that are not too stiff. I might also do some gym work which will help strengthen legs, thighs and calves – some light weights, and some skipping.

I will work very hard for five days. On the sixth I play squash for two or three hours and on the seventh there is complete rest. Then it is wise to get completely away from squash and perhaps even from one's usual environment. I never recommend training every day. Keep one for recharging the battery.

All Round Strength

Training should be aimed to improve the legs, stomach, arms, mind, and heart. Legs should be built up all round. A lot of players make the mistake of building them at the front or the back, and trouble can then follow. If one muscle is weak and another strong, this may stretch and take the weak one with it, and tear it. These days there are gymnasiums with charts that show you which muscles to work on. Look at these before building the muscles up.

We don't need big muscles for squash. Therefore use light weight exercises with plenty of repetition. For legs use gymwork, for arms use hitting the ball or swinging the racket in shadow exercises: one minute forehand, one minute backhand, one minute volley, one minute overhead. Sometimes you can do this with the racket cover on. It builds up the forearms.

It is particularly important if you do this to finish off by hitting the ball or you will tend to lose control of your strokes. For similar reasons I don't approve of press-ups for squash players. I much prefer pull-ups where you can grip and let go of your body, strengthening both the grip and the arm. With press-ups the weight is all on your hands with too much pressure on them. This will not help your control for whatever you subsequently do.

A good exercise to reproduce the movements of running for a drop shot is to run forwards for fifty yards, backwards for fifty yards, sideways for fifty, and then running and touching the ground. Then try running and jumping up in the air (as if for a volley) and then hopping on one leg. All the movements are like those in a rally. A straight run builds up one set of muscles at one rhythm.

One way to introduce variety is to have a trainer kick the ball away as far as he can. You then run, pick it up, and bring it back, and he kicks it again without the player knowing where it is going, sometimes short, sometimes long. Again these are like squash movements. They are also useful for motivation because one gets fed up with the same kind of training all the time. They occupy the mind.

At other times I do a sprint, then sit down, and get up and spring again, covering a length of ground that way. I then retrace my steps by jumping up in the air when coming up into the sprinting position. These once again reproduce the movements for the drop shot and high volley.

On Court Exercises

On court I will sit down at the back, get up and sprint to the front and then return to the back wall again, to face it. Then I get up, turn and repeat the same thing, except that this time I lie down on my chest. The third time I lie on my back. In squash matches your body often relaxes and then tenses up for sudden activity. These exercises create something similar.

I also do a great deal of running and jumping over other persons. This is good for the motivation when the legs are tired. Having someone else there always makes you work harder. When I was really tired at the end of a session I would sometimes run carrying a person on my back. If you can take that for five hundred yards you are building up something extra. At the end of training I would also often do skipping.

There is one other very good training exercise that I didn't really want to reveal. I had to be persuaded. It is an outstandingly good circuit training, done three ways, for legs, stomach, and arms.

To start with, the player runs ten times to the front wall and back again in order to bring his pulse rate high (obviously though he has to be warmed up to do that). After that he does one exercise for the legs, whatever exercise he likes. Then he sprints twice to the front wall and back: two sprints between every exercise. Next he does an exercise for the stomach, perhaps sit-ups. Next one for the arms, perhaps racket swinging. Each time two sprints in between. Do twenty or thirty of those and you'll become a very fit player. I tell myself that it's not the players who read about these things who will be dangerous, it's the ones who go out and actually do them. There won't be many of those.

Forethought

About half of players' injury and health problems can be prevented by forethought. The day of rest will also help prevent a breakdown. So will meticulous warming up and warming down exercises, removing wet clothes quickly, showering at the correct temperature and drying your hair properly. Don't stand around talking to people after matches or training. These are small tips, but few players observe them all without fail.

If you get a problem or an injury, go to the physiotherapist; if you get a nasty cold or feel bad, go to the doctor. Even if you can sometimes sweat through a cold it is better not to take risks. Regular check-ups are necessary. You should know how your heart and lungs are holding up. And if you know something is wrong, as Torsam did, you should be honest about it, and not risk playing.

You must also prepare yourself mentally. Squash requires you to perform under great physical stress, never to give up, and yet, at the same time, to conduct yourself decently towards your opponent, the marker and the referee. As if that were not enough, you must accept and learn from defeat, adapt and go on. You must also conduct yourself in a respectable manner off the court, in order to help promote the game, to be loyal to sponsors, and to be a credit to yourself.

These things are not at all easy. You will need to build yourself up. You will need a dialogue with someone about difficulties, which is why it will assist you to have helpers and a philosophy. At different times I have had Rahmat Khan, Umar Draz Khan, and my father Roshan Khan. I also had Islam. There are other forms of support – yoga, meditation, hypnotherapy, relaxation exercises – all of which I have talked about.

Attitude

What I want to stress, finally, is the degree of effort that must come from inside *you*. It is you who must do these things, coach, philosophy, religion or not. It is no good saying, 'God make me win!' Nor must your attitude to any kind of support be to get something for nothing. You can only ask for the strength of mind to use help properly. Once you have done this, and accepted your responsibility in it, then all sorts of acknowledgements, and sometimes miracles, can occur.

Though the effort has to come from you, I also want to convince you that the ability to trigger it probably exists inside you. The next world champion will have to have a mixture of great strokes, great fitness and great mental qualities all together. It is not impossible. What so many people don't realize is the tremendous well of inspiration and energy that exists within each of us. Such people have to decide that this reservoir is worth seeking; after that there are always ways of succeeding. I hope this book may help you find some of them.

APPENDIX 1: PARTS OF THE SQUASH COURT

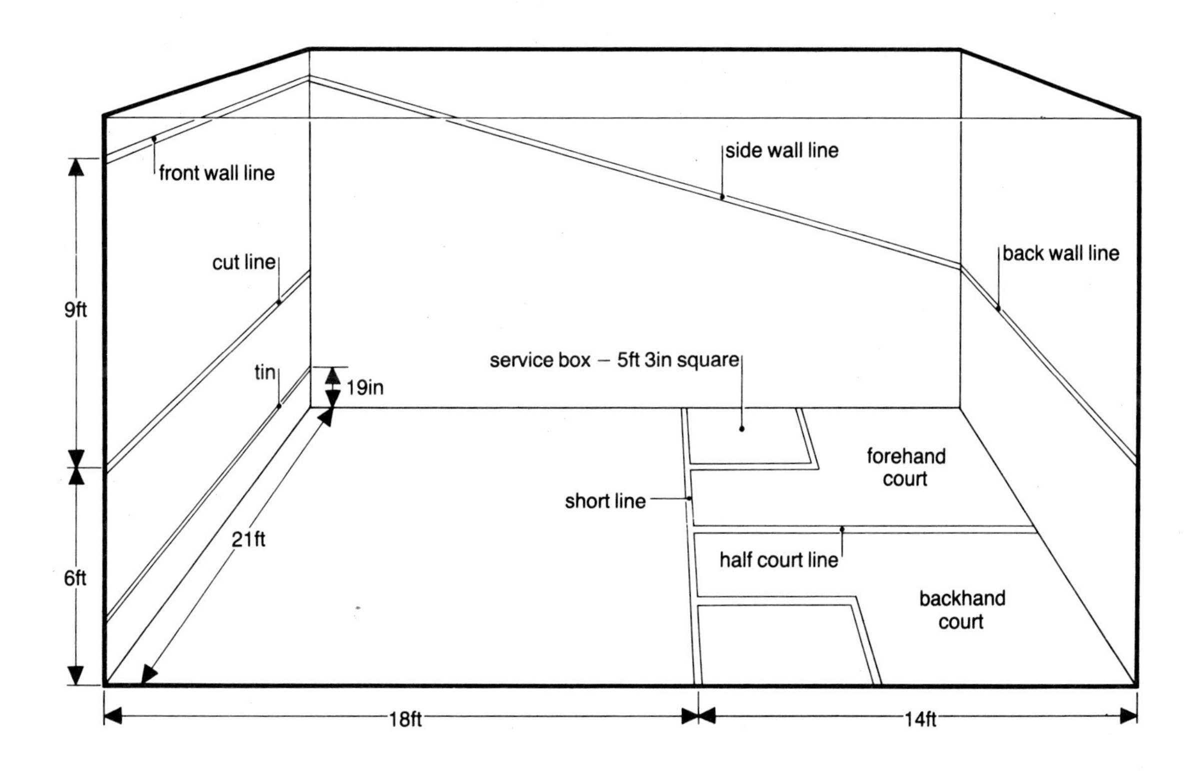